It's All HIS Fault

THE BLAME GAME ... THE RIGHT WAY

RUBY E. POWELL

Unless otherwise indicated, all scripture quotations, references and definitions are from the Authorized King James Version © 1987; The New King James Version © 1982 by Thomas Nelson, Inc.; The New International Version 1973, 1978, 1984 by International Bible Society by the Zondervan Corporation; The Amplified Bible Old Testament © 1962, 1964, 1965, 1987 by the Zondervan Corporation; The Amplified New Testament © 1954, 1958, 1987 by the Lockman Foundation; The Message. Copyright © 1993, 1994, 1995, 1996, 2000, 2001, 2002. Used by permission of NavPress Publishing Group. All rights reserved; M.G. Easton M.A., D.D., Illustrated Bible Dictionary, Third Edition, published by Thomas Nelson, 1897; The Name Book © 1982, 1997 by Dorothy Astoria.

ITS ALL HIS/HER FAULT
The Blame Game The Right Way

Tony & Ruby Powell
tonyandruby@theblamegame.us
855-627-4748

Copyright © 2019 by Tony & Ruby Powell

ISBN 978-1-943342-42-6

Designed & Published by
PublishAffordably.com • 773.783.2981

Dedications

This book is dedicated to the memory of our spiritual mother, the late Apostle Jo Ann Long of *Let's Talk About Marriage and the Family* and to our spiritual father, Dr. John T. Long of *Adam Where Art Thou?* You all gave us a solid foundation for marriage and was dedicated to praying for our success.

To our natural parents, Porter C. Powell, the Late Elouise Powell (continue to rest in heaven), R.D. Roberson, and Mattie Williams. You all gave us life and taught us tenacity. Without tenacity, there are some days that we would have thrown in the towel. Thank you for always having our back.

To the Tribe of Powell (#TOPChronicles): our gifted, talented, and selfless children, Adya Monique, Kasiya Janae, Nathan Joseph Anthony, and Jonathan Christian. We can't thank you all enough for sacrificing so much of your time to allow us to minister to others; you recognize the value of what we are doing. We're thankful that God always make it up to you all!

To all of the relationships that will be helped as a result of our vulnerability and transparency.

It's All *His* Fault - The Blame Game The Right Way

Acknowledgements

We will not dare start to name all of our friends that encouraged us to write this book, you all know who you are!! We love you with all of our heart!

To our Pastors and friends, Jerry and Chris McQuay. Thank you for receiving us so lovingly into the family of Christian Life Center – Tinley Park and trusting us to serve as Elders in the church. We love you all tremendously!

To our writing team, Dr. Alice Maria Crawford, JoAnna Wilson, John and Deborah Anthony. Thank you for enduring the crunch time reading and solid feedback. To Marilyn Alexander ~ you have been telling us for the last several years that we had to get this done and held our feet to the fire until it was done!

Contents

This book is a step by step account of how we met, married, and survived the challenges of marriage. We recognized how our upbringing and the examples of marriage that we witnessed formed unhealthy thoughts and marital behaviors.

Through good solid counseling and study of the Bible, we were able to develop a healthy respect for each other that formed a system for how to "place blame" in a more positive manner.

The 4-B Principle (Be Prayerful, Be Patient, Be Proactive, and Be Permanent) give detailed instruction on how to resolve conflict and create relationships that are enjoyable, productive, and fulfilling life.

It Started In Prayer, Literally

I guess my story goes kind of like this! I was the youngest of four children born to my parents in the Altgeld Gardens community, which sits on the border of Chicago and Riverdale, IL. Altgeld Gardens was a low-income housing project that consisted of townhouses and row houses. We had no clue that we lived in low-income housing because the community was well cared for and the residents took excellent care of their property. The lawns were well manicured and adorned with flower beds.

All of the neighborhood parents took responsibility for each other's children. There was no such thing as a child disrespecting an adult; even the 'gangbangers' stopped cursing and fussing when they saw an adult approaching. Regardless of who the child was and their social status in the community, the parents taught the children to respect their elders. Disagreements among children would be settled quickly, sometimes ending in a fist fight, but by sundown they were right back to playing and laughing like nothing ever happened. Totally unheard of, right? This was not uncommon for the 1960s.

I would describe our family as typical for the times that we lived in. The majority of my friends lived in two-parent households, with the father as the primary breadwinner and a stay-at-home mother. My parents had four other couples that they regularly socialized with. The children of my parents' friends became our friends. Our weekends consisted of Friday night Bid Whist games at someone's house.

The women would start frying chicken and fish early in the day because when the husbands came home from work, the Bid Whist games would start shortly thereafter. The kids would play in the courtyard area until late into the evening while those card games were going on. The parents were in their own world—and so were the kids! The kids would pass out at each other's houses until the next morning because the Bid Whist games would usually go on all night long!

On Saturdays, after the parents retrieved their children and completed normal Saturday chores, the families would pile in their big old cars—our was a huge red Pontiac Bonneville— and go to the drive-in movie in Riverdale, IL. We were one big happy family that consisted of the Robersons, the Taylor/ Loves, the Battles, the Andersons, and the Gardeners. Sunday mornings consisted of us going to church. I don't really remember being involved in many of the church's activities, but my mother would make sure that she took us to church. Sunday afternoons were reserved for family picnics, trips to Riverview Amusement Park, Santa's Village, and any other things we could do for entertainment before the weekday activities started again. Our family truly enjoyed spending time with our friends and with each other.

During the week, we lived the "Leave it to Beaver" type life of Dad going off to work, Mom taking care of the household, and us going off to Carver Elementary School. Dad was the quintessential provider. He sometimes worked two or three jobs to make sure that there was always a roof over our head and food on the table. He worked a variety of jobs until he fell into his ultimate dream career as a photographer. He worked as a commercial photographer, taking pictures for print catalogs such as J.C. Penney, Sears, and Montgomery Wards. By evening, he was an electrician, television repairman, and freelance photographer.

Mom always made sure that we had hot, homemade meals (dinner was always complete with homemade desserts of peach cobbler, pound cake, banana pudding, etc.—oh mercy, I digress!). My mother made all of our clothes; at one point she even became a milliner, making hats for people. We were some of the best-dressed kids in the neighborhood, although she always dressed my sister and I alike. We didn't really like it because we were not twins, like our older brothers. She was the PTA parent and field trip chaperone, all while keeping the house spotless, clothes cleaned and pressed, and meals prepared. I'm getting tired just thinking about all that my parents did to keep our family strong!

As the American dream was being discovered by many of the families, the migration from Altgeld Gardens began to occur. Slowly, each of the families saved enough money to buy houses in Chicago. We moved from Altgeld Gardens in July of 1970 into the home where I spent the remainder of my childhood (my dad still lives in that house). We managed to maintain those relationships for a while as new relationships began to form in our new neighborhood. The Friday night card parties became less and less common over time; instead of being weekly, now they occurred about once a month, eventually stopping altogether. The Saturday drive-in movies were not the same without our "family" of kids running from car to car, never really watching the movie. We had to adjust to a new way of life and living! These friendships formed a foundation of what relationships would look like for the rest my life. My expectation was that all friends were close knit the way our Altgeld Family was. Our family did form very close relationships after our move—some that we still maintain.

My dad continued to work two or three jobs to support the increased responsibilities of being a new homeowner. He worked his regular day job as a commercial photographer but also built a dark room and a workbench in the basement of our home. In the dark room, he processed pictures from his freelance photography work, and on the workbench he repaired televisions and other small electronics.

My mom continued to care for the home and family. She still enjoyed sewing and cooking and being actively involved in our school activities. Mom began taking us to church on a regular basis and getting us involved in the activities that were offered there. At different points, we were at church whenever the church doors opened. My mom did a lot of volunteer work at the church; this volunteer work became an outlet for her. After a while, my mom began to pursue outside employment. I'm not sure whether it was due to the financial need of the family, but that change, as I saw it, became a huge turning point in our peaceful family life. All of a sudden, our "Leave it to Beaver" family began to crumble.

One day my parents announced to the four of us that they were separating. My mother was moving out! This was earth shattering, to say the least. Just to put things in context, it was a major shocker because we never, ever heard our parents argue or disagree. They did such an amazing job of insulating us from any form of disturbance, so that made the news of separation seem inconceivable! As the baby of the family, I prided myself on being the favorite of both of my parents (my siblings would probably disagree). I never saw it coming! This occurred at a pivotal point in all of our lives. My brothers were young adults trying to figure out how to become men, my sister was a pregnant high school senior, and I was in 8th grade.

Please understand that it is never my intention to place shame or blame on anyone, especially not my parents. Sometimes it is important to reveal things in order to heal from them. Some of these life-changing events shaped how I interacted in and viewed relationships for a large part of my teenage and young adult years. I instinctively took responsibility for the destruction of my family—I should have seen it coming, I should have been able to do something about this. I began a pathway to personal destruction that would last for most of my teenage years and into my early adulthood. During the last year of my parents' marriage, I became involved in a relationship with a young man that was five years older than me. I was in 8th grade and he had already graduated from high school. My parents allowed the relationship because he was a very polite and well-mannered young man (what were they thinking!). Of course, I thought I was doing something big because I had an older boyfriend. Well at 13 years old, what did I even know about relationships or love other than the example of my parents and other marriages around me? And many of those marriages were falling apart.

I became acutely aware that the reality of my younger years with a two-parent families was now very different. I remember my brother trying to comfort me about my parents' separation by pointing out all of the other marriages of our friends that were also breaking up. During the four years of that intermittent relationship, I experienced things that caused me to become calloused and cold regarding relationships.

For the first time in my life, I experienced the perpetuation of rejection, which led to so many other negative emotions and behaviors. I began to look for and find "love" in all the wrong places. Unfortunately, I didn't have anyone that could guide, correct, or direct me away from these relationships. Over the next 15 years or so, I subjected myself to one unproductive relationship after another, which were unhealthy and completely against the will of God for my life.

The part that I left out was that I had stopped going to church when my parents separated because somehow I blamed God and the church for not protecting the sanctity of my family. I went on a binge of self-destructive behaviors, which included me doing anything that I was big and bad enough to do without any regard for the outcome. My reign of self-destruction lasted approximately 10 years, until I decided one Sunday to just stop by the church that I grew up in. Time seemed to stand still—things were exactly the same as I had left them 10 years prior. God is so amazing that he kept me cocooned in Him until I came to myself. After a few Sundays of sneaking in the back of the church after service started and leaving before it was over, I realized that I needed the safety and security of a relationship with God. I continued to come to church Sunday after Sunday until the guilt and shame of all of the things that I had done began to wash away. Eventually, I felt the urge to participate in church activities again. This time I thought my perspective about life and church people was different because I was no longer a vulnerable kid that could be hurt by people's actions or inactions. Over years of being out of church, I had developed a calloused and hard shell that would not let any love out or any love in. Although I was going through the motions of being in church and even participating, I did not allow the love of God to penetrate my heart. I led what I would later realize was a double life: my church life and my personal life. Who was I kidding! I even began working for the church as the church secretary/administrator.

The real wakeup call came when I found myself unmarried and pregnant at the age of 28 by one of my childhood best friends—a story for a whole different book. There I was, a youth leader in my church, teaching the youth to be chaste and "religious," but now I was pregnant. Shame, guilt, embarrassment, condemnation, frustration, disappointment, anger, and failure all showed up at my door once again. How would I explain this to my youth, my pastor…my parents! For the first time in my life, I cried out to the God that I had always heard about, had read about, but had never experienced personally. I needed help! I needed forgiveness! I needed so many more things that I didn't realize that I needed. I needed a real relationship with God but didn't know how to get it. My daughter, Adya Monique, was born in September of 1991. Becoming responsible for another whole life changed me forever. I knew that there were many things about me that had to change; my thinking had to change, my behavior had to change, and my spirit had to change. I continued to cry out to God like never before, and to my surprise, He heard me! He began to help me in ways that I would not recognize until many years later. I still held myself in condemnation and guilt because no one had yet taught me that I could repent and God would forgive me and even allow me to forgive myself.

Rewinding life to the summer of 1987, Tony and I had a chance meeting when he and his singing partner Sheila were singing at a wedding that I was in at their church. It was very casual meeting that went something like this, "Hey Ruby, this is Pastor Tony"! "Hi Pastor Tony, nice to meet you!" Only God knows why the bride felt the need to introduce us at that moment.

A lot happened in my life from that day to the next time I saw him in 1999 when he began attending the church that I was then a member of. When I saw him, his face looked familiar but I had no idea why! Later I heard that he was a pretty famous guy because he had written some songs, was a regular on TV38 (a once popular Christian TV station in Chicago), and was in a couple of movies! So, I just assumed that was why his face looked familiar. He then became the Director of Program Operations at the church. During the time, I was transitioning from one career assignment to another and had about a 4-month gap when I was not working. Our church had 8 am prayer every morning ~ well, that's when it started in prayer! Every morning after dropping my daughter off at school, I would go to the church and pray with the other intercessory prayers for an hour; many days I would stay and pray for a few hours longer.

There is a saying "what you make happen for others, God will make happen for you!" Only God knows the thoughts and intents of my heart. I say that at this point because at that time, I had not been involved in a dating relationship for 10 years. Dating was the furthest thing from my mind ~ much less marriage. Honestly, I was building my career, furthering my education, raising my daughter as a single parent, and spending as much time with God as I could. I had long since lost my desire to be married because I felt like it was just another thing to do. I had been involved in enough relationships that did not lead to marriage and some that ended rather bitterly.

Secondly, I hadn't seen many, if any, successful examples of marriage during my lifetime. Most of the people around me that were married were having problem and asking me to pray for them (some even asked me to counsel them because of my degree in counseling ~ who am I to counsel married folks having never been married). Needless to say, I would pray and ask God to restore their love for each other, to allow them to find the love that they once had for each other, that they would have a desire to stay together and to fight for their marriage. As I was praying for those couples, I had no idea that God was softening my heart for relationship and ultimately marriage. The hurt and pain of past relationships that had caused a callous on my heart was being chipped away as I prayed to see marriages healed.

As the Director of Program Operations, Minister Powell (as he was known) was there to open the doors and provide security for the women that came in to pray each morning. He was always so nice and friendly but one day as I was leaving the church after being in prayer for about three and a half hours, I walked past his office, he spoke and asked what kind of work I did. I guess he was wondering why I had so much time on my hands. He mentioned how professional I was and he was just curious as to what business I was in. He noted the work that I did in the church as well as working closely alongside my pastor.

That morning, I stood in his office door and talked to him for about an hour and a half about business and ministry. I was so naïve not knowing that he was kind of flirting with me ~ I guess. I had not been flirted with in a long time so my flirting meter was really, really rusty! I remember saying to him the next day that I enjoyed our conversation; I promise you I wasn't flirting but I had isolated myself for so long that I didn't know what a real genuine conversation was like. I had turned my ears off to the old "pickup lines" that I would hear in the streets.

I had no idea that what he noticed and admired most about me was my prayer life and the relationship that I had with God. He later told me that he knew that I was able to love and take care for my daughter the way that I did because of my intimate relationship with God. He also commented on how well I regarded my pastor/spiritual mom! Why was it all his fault… he was perceptive enough to know that the old standard pickup lines were not going to work with me!

The Journey Together Begins

During the next few months, we had casual hi and bye conversations in passing. Valentine's Day rolled around and Minister Powell gave me a very subtle Valentine day card and inside the card was a crisp $50 bill with a note that said, 'Take your daughter to dinner on me!' I was mortified, frightened, petrified, and a myriad of other fright-filled emotions. Why you may ask! Well remember I had not been in a relationship in 10 years.

I didn't know what he was thinking or implying. I checked myself to make sure I wasn't sending out the wrong signals. Did he think I liked him? Did he think that I was interested in a relationship with him? God, oh God, oh my God ~ what was really going on! I started saying I should have never talked to him that day a few months before. When I tell you that I was a total basket case. I was afraid to tell anyone about the card because they would immediately think that I had led him on. The devil really knew how to play tricks on my mind. Boy was that the longest 12 hours until the next 8 am prayer.

The next morning, I couldn't get to prayer fast enough. I ran in the door to the church, straight to his office, and gave him the card back. He didn't understand why I was giving it back so I started babbling about how I don't take money from men and that I don't know what kind of women he thought I was. I went on to say that I don't know what this means and what he expected from me. He looked at me and laughed so hard. If you have ever heard my husband laugh it is not one that you would soon forget. As I continued to babble and he continued to laugh, I immediately started feeling like the biggest idiot. Why was he laughing at me!! Dog-gone-it, I was serious! I was living a life of Christ and I was sold out and I refused to return to playing Russian roulette with my soul! I did the thing that heightened the drama already building ~ yes, I started crying! I had worked myself into a panic and a frenzy!

After he stopped laughing, he patiently explained to me that he saw how well I took care of my daughter and just thought it would be a nice gesture to treat us to dinner. No strings or no expectations attached! Boy, did I feel like the biggest fool. Although I still did not want to take the card, I asked my best friend what I should do! She said, Girl take that baby to Red Lobster (my daughter's former babysitter got her hooked on Red Lobster when she was about 2 years old).

I guess he thought I was a little crazy because he didn't really say a whole lot to me after that. I was still rather embarrassed at my tirade and meltdown that whenever I passed by him, I dropped my head when I spoke. Little did I know, he laid in wait, continuing to observe my spiritual behavior and posture because he saw something different in me than some of the other women in the church. So many of women in the church gravitated to him because not only was he incredibly gifted, talented, and anointed as a Psalmist and Musician but he was also extremely charismatic. His silky-smooth singing and speaking voice caused people, especially women to pay attention. Many of them sought his attention and even expressed an interest in him romantically. I, on the other hand, was running as fast as I could in the other direction.

In addition to the fact that I was not interested in dating anyone, there were a couple of things that didn't interest me about him. At the time that he came to our church he was a married man. I was really not interested in a married man at all. I hadn't noticed that his wife had long since stop coming to church with him. I was not subject to church gossip so I just didn't know or notice that he was no longer attached.

One of his many talents in working at the church was that he engineered my pastor's radio program, Let's Talk about Marriage and the Family every day. We would encounter each other on a regular basis as I worked very closely as an assistant to her. He would go out of his way to speak to me and say nice things to me, so much so that others began to notice and tell me, I think Minister Powell like you. All I could think to myself was, why don't he leave me alone. I finally told one young lady that mentioned that on multiple occasions that she was so dead wrong because he already had a wife and pastor would not stand for such foolishness in the church. This young lady said to me, "His wife has not been to church in over 6 months and I think they are no longer together. That still didn't move me!! I was still uninterested!!

It was true that he and his wife had separated and during the time that he was engineering the Let's Talk about Marriage and the Family show, he was receiving counsel, wisdom, and getting healed from not his first, but his second failed marriage. He had sworn to God that he would never marry again because he had failed at it twice. Those were his exact words to our pastor. She repeatedly told him, "Powell, God don't want to you be alone. You are supposed to be married! God has a good wife for you!" After a while, he told her that there was a young lady in the church that was of interest to him. As he began to tell her who it was and why he was so intrigued, her first response was, "Powell, let me pray!" I'm not sure whether she was shocked or concerned. I was like a daughter to her and she just didn't know whether that could or would work! What she did know was that he was not ready to begin the journey to dating again; he still had much more work to do to completely heal.

As he continued to demonstrate that he was ready to move forward with his life, still not convinced that he wanted to marry again, she agreed to allow him to pursue me. Mind you, this is over a year after that first conversation. She placed strict parameters on the process because she was intentional about guarding me as her spiritual daughter and making sure that he had eliminated enough baggage to not wound me. Ole naïve me still didn't know what was going on because his approach was slow and deliberate. He finally asked if he could take me and my daughter to dinner. Well, don't you know I panicked again. My first respond was, "For what!" He said, "To eat!" At that time, I heard a voice from heaven (it could have only been from heaven) say, "That is your husband!"

After I told him to let me think about it, I went into vehement protest with God. I told him all the reasons why he couldn't be my husband! He wasn't my type, he had been married before (I would later learn that it was twice before), there were so many others that were vying for his attention (I didn't want the drama). As I was whining and bellyaching with God, He reminded me that I had a baby out of wedlock ~ Wow, God did you have to remind me of that! He didn't remind me of my unwed mother status to condemn me but to remind me that I had no right to condemn anyone else or to denounce what He was pronouncing!

And Now The Rest Is History...

God began to soften my heart and let me know that I was capable of receiving love just like I freely gave love! Over the course of the next year (really mostly clandestinely) we began to get to know one another. We were very careful to follow the dating regulations of our pastor. You may not think that is important because we were both very grown! I was 38 years of age and he was 43 years old when the relationship began to blossom. It was so important to me that if the Lord was to sanction our relationship, that we would be intentional about dating His way and since our pastor was the one that was responsible for watching for our souls, we submitted to her guidance. When I tell you, the struggle was real, not in the dating relationship because he was the perfect gentleman at all times, but in my mindset.

God began to change my focus to seeing the example that my pastor put before me in marriage. She and her husband never pretended that their marriage was perfect but that they were invested in each other. That was enough for me! I began to voice to her how fearful I was about wanting to prepare myself for the role of being a wife! I began to see how God used the prior 10 years of my life to transform me into what he designed my life to be as a wife, mother, lover, nurturer, incubator of his dreams, entrepreneur, all while continuing his work in my life.

As we were dating, I was very careful to protect my daughter. She had never witness her mom being involved in a relationship. We dated for about six months before I allowed him to come to the home that I shared with my 9-year-old daughter. Tony and I had a conversation with her to explain that we "like" each other a lot and that we would be engaging in a dating relationship. We let her know that she would be a very special part of this relationship. We also assured her that we would never disrespect her in any way. I later assured her that she could talk to me at any time about Tony and my relationship. She then asked me if she could call him Uncle Tony!! I was shocked as I really thought she would rebel against having to share her mom with someone else. She was a part of every date that we went on and whenever he visited our home she was always present. That was important for a number of reasons.

My daughter and Uncle Tony began to form a special bond that would later turn into a real father-daughter relationship. I began to meet members of Tony's family and he began to meet members of my family. We were still not very forthcoming with being seen together at church at that time. He remained respectful of my hesitancy to date, especially since he was so popular at church! He didn't try to push me into developing full trust in him nor did he pressure me to go public with our relationship. Honestly, I believe that he was a little afraid too. He continued to receive counsel and guidance from our pastor as he was relentless in his quest to do marriage right this time. Tony worked behind the scenes to make sure that he had the full support of my family.

At the appointed time, the time that our pastor said was appropriate, he purchased an engagement ring and gave it to our pastor for safekeeping. He gave it her because he had found the perfect ring but the timing for proposing had not yet come. I didn't know until after we married that my daughter knew about the ring and was excited about it. Uncle Tony was about to become Daddy!! That's also when I learned that my daughter could keep a secret ~ she didn't say a word about the ring or his intentions.

During the next few months, Tony also got to know my dad really well. At that time, my dad lived in the house next door to me so whenever Tony came by to pick us up, he would often see my very protective dad. One weekend Tony decided that it would be nice if my family and his family went to breakfast one Saturday morning. So, we ALL (my daughter, my dad, his sisters, their children, his mother…everybody) met at a nice buffet restaurant for breakfast. As we were moving around the restaurant eating and going back and forth to the buffet, I noticed that Tony was having a very intense conversation with my dad at the table. It was one of those conversations that you just don't interrupt. Tony was asking my dad for my hand in marriage. Who does that!!!! By that time, he was 44 years old and I was 39! I will tell you that his stock really went up with me! I began to think that maybe he wasn't so bad after all and that this may be able to work out.

With all systems go, pastor approved – check; daughter approved – check; dad approved – check … on December 23, 2002 during the church's Christmas concert, Tony finally asked ME if he could have my hand in marriage. The church went into an exuberant shout as I stared like a deer looking into headlights. I didn't know what to do … what did I do … I said yes and on May 31, 2003 we became Minister and Mrs. Anthony Powell.

Why was it all his fault… because he did it all right! He honored God, he honored our spiritual leaders, he honored my daughter, he honored by dad as my covering which means that he honored ME!

What's Really In You, Will Come Out!

Let me digress to the engagement process, I was still petrified because I now had a status that I had never had before. I was soon to be a wife. What I was really clear about was that at the age of 39, I didn't have time for a super long engagement so I had to get ready quickly. There was a lot to do and very little time to do it. We wouldn't dare set a date to get married until we had begun pre-marital counsel. In my mind, not only was pre-marital counsel mandatory but it gave me an opportunity to get to know more about this man that I knew very little about.

We started our premarital counseling right away with our senior pastor's husband (my spiritual father). Prior to meeting my husband, my spiritual father was one of the two men in my life that protected me. He was even more protective than my biological father!! As a matter of fact, during our first premarital session, he asked my then fiancé, "Powell, what are your intentions toward Ruby?" I chuckled for a couple of different reasons! First, I was shocked that he asked that question. I don't know that my biological father even asked that. As Powell, spat and sputtered trying to answer the question, I sat back like thinking "Yeah, let him have it!" He told my fiancé, "I better not ever see her come in here crying because you mistreated or didn't honor her!"

Then it was my turn to spit and sputter as I tried to answer the question, "Ruby, what are you bringing to the table?" All I could think to answer was all of the things that I had accomplished that really had nothing to do with being successful in marriage ~ after all, I didn't know what I was supposed to bring to the table. Unlike all of my years of professional studies, I had not taken the time to study the art of marriage. As I said earlier, my only frames of reference were broken marriages and couples who lived together without marrying; both of which I wanted no part of. The rest of that session was a blur as I realized this was really happening, my status was changing and I had better change with it. I began to pray that God would help me to get ready to all that "this" meant. It was all happening so fast!

During the next premarital session with our pastor and her husband, we began to talk about a variety of things some of which were his previous marriages, my previous relationships, how to resolve conflict, how to co-parent, and other subjects that could be difficult in a new marriage. My pastor asked me, "Ruby, are you ready for this?" I then said words that had to come straight from God because not only did I have no idea where they came from but I didn't even know what those words meant! I said, "Mom, I am anointed to be married to him!" Oh no, where did that come from! What did I just say! What does that mean! A hush came over the room for which seemed like an eternity. My pastor (my spiritual mother) finally broke the silent and said, "Baby, God will help you!" I guess she saw the look of horror on my face. I will later realize what those words actually meant!

There were things that happened along the way from January 2003 through May 31, 2003 that made me question my readiness for this forever journey but God kept reminding me that I was anointed for this. My flesh and my spirit had a real fight! Honestly, I still didn't want to get married because I didn't want to give up my freedom. Up until that point, I was free to come and go as I please! The only person that I had to consider with my comings and goings, was my daughter! I was very protective of her so I was conscious to never do anything that would discredit me in her eyes. Now I have to start considering another person in my comings and goings. I also didn't want to have to share my space and my possessions! Wow, I certainly had a lot to learn! I didn't feel like I could ask anyone about my fears or trepidations. You see, on the outside, I looked like I had it all together; my outward appearance exuded confidence but on the inside I was a mess! What's on the inside will definitely come out.

After our premarital counseling was done and it was time to set a date, I told my pastor that I was ready to get the license and get married. I was content with getting married in a very small, private ceremony in her office. She had a way of looking at me and looking through me at the same time. I recognized that look as a look of disapproval at what I had just shared. She asked me why I felt that way to which I gave some lame answer about how I didn't want to be bothered with planning and stuff! Of course, she wasn't buying that. She said to me that every woman deserves to be a bride. I had sense enough to know that there was more to what she was saying than I heard that day. She was such a deep thinker and such a great woman of wisdom ~ I knew that would not be the end of that discussion.

As I was helping her with a task one day she started to talk about inner vows that people make. She said some startling things that begin to make me think about my life and why I processed things the way I did. I had been a single mother for 10 years and always felt like I had to figure out things on my own. Before that, I had to learn some adult lessons at a young age.

My parents separated and divorced when I was 14 years old after 19 years of marriage. I lived with my father from then until I moved out on my own at 23. My dad was a true provider! All of my young memories of my dad were of him working one, two, or three jobs to provide for his family. So, I had to learn how to keep a house, write checks to pay bills, balance a check book, plan and cook meals, grocery shop, etc … all those things it took to run a household all while going to high school. I don't say any of this to blame or shame anyone but simply to explain some of the inner vows that I made that caused me to think and live beneath my privileges as a King's daughter! Those early experiences caused me to develop some bitterness that I pushed to the back of my mind while I built a defensive wall. I never really knew that I was not okay! I was moving forward and accomplishing great things in my education, my career, my parenting but I was stuck! My feet were in quicksand.

As I talked with my pastor that day, she told me some things that God had showed her about me and my past that I never really shared with anyone. That day she very lovingly walked me through my escape from self-imposed bondage. There were no signs, wonders, miracles, lightning bolts; just pure love and understanding. See, I had convinced myself that I was not worthy of anything good! How could that be since I appeared to be successful on every front ~ I had advanced educational degrees, I had a middle management executive position with the state, I had purchased my own home, I was driving a new car every couple of years (and paying them off), my daughter had always attended private school, we took nice vacations every year (I also took vacations by myself for a break from parenting) ... yet, I was broken. I was angry with my parents for separating and divorcing. That set the course for me looking at every other couple that was not married or had been married and divorced!

In my mind, I was good but I was not. So, after I begin to process my anger and bitterness, I realized that I had set a barrier that caused me to not want to marry. But I was engaged, right!?! Yep, and since God said that I should be married and that this was my husband, I said, no wedding, let's just get it over with so I can operate in this anointing that I was told that I had to be married to Tony Powell! Even after all of that, I wasn't convinced that I wanted a wedding. I had convinced myself that if I could not have the wedding that I dreamed of as a little girl that I didn't want one. My pastor very clearly and sternly told me that if I didn't have a wedding, that she would not marry us. WHAT!! I couldn't allow someone else to marry us!! I allowed God to begin the healing process and agreed to have a wedding.

I can honestly say now that I would have greatly regretted not having a wedding. We took three and a half months to plan our May 31st fairy tale wedding. Our wedding was compared to the wedding on the movie Coming to America. I felt like a Queen as I walked down the aisle of my church from the arm of my dad to the arms of my husband. Our marriage was witnessed by about 500 guest. We had two receptions ~ a nice upscale hors 'oeuvres reception at the church and then a sit-down reception for about 200. Everything fell into place! Our entire wedding and both receptions were completely paid for before we even got to the wedding day! That was a miracle… supernatural! We can't figure out to this day how that happened! It really was only God's doing!

So again, you ask, why was it all his fault ~ because he allowed God to put him right in my path to help me to get free from so many things that held me back.

"OMG
The Vows Get Tested"

Some couple write their own wedding vows because they want to be fancy and they have special things that they want to say to each other. I often wonder do they really know what they are saying and do they fully intend to keep those vows. In the blur of the moment during the wedding ceremony, we say those fateful words, whether personal or traditional, that typically end in "I DO". Do we still remember those exact words 5, 10, 15 years down the line? Are those words still true? You make those vows in the presence of witnesses, whether 5 or 500, but your vows are really between you, your spouse, and God!

With what you know now about your spouse, do you still mean I do? Did you really mean for better or worse, for richer or for poorer, in sickness and in health… till death do us part?? Or did you until the worse comes, until we have some serious financial needs, until one of us gets really sick… even if I have to kill you? That may sound a little humorous but when we say those vows, in most cases we really don't expect to have to live them out ~ at least I didn't! I was 40 years old when I got married and I've already talked about how I thought I had it all together. Well at the age of 45, I thought my soon to be husband had it all together too! Boy was I in for a big surprise!

Couples may say those vows blindly because in many cases there are so many things that we don't know about our intended spouse. Even when couples live together prior to marriage there seems to be something that changes when they flip that "I do" switch. All of a sudden, things that were previously okay or tolerable seems to now be an annoyance, things that were suspicions soon become reality. You find yourself saying, "Wow, how did I miss that?"

For Better or For Worse

Statistics say that the hardest time in any marital relationship is the first year. That seems to make sense especially since the couple is trying to get to know each other in a different, more intimate way. If you never lived with your spouse, you don't know that they leave the top off the toothpaste or they leave dishes in the sink at night or they leave their underwear and everything else on the floor or that they are a neat freak.

I thought I had prepared myself for living with another adult person because of the stories that I had heard. I was good with those things. I figured that I would just show him how it should be done. The saying that you can't teach an old dog new tricks is so true when it comes to marriage. Women sometimes see things that they don't like and instinctively tell themselves that it will change or that they will change their spouse. Men don't seem to care about some of the obnoxious behaviors of their spouse but certainly don't want to feel like they are sleeping with their mother.

Our story was slightly different! Our worse year was not our first year, or our second year, or our third year. By the third year I thought we were sailing smooth. I had such a false sense of security and remember saying so many times, "this is not so bad! I can do this until death do us part." Until all of a sudden, we hit an iceberg! Why do I say an iceberg? Well if you know the nature of an iceberg, you see a portion on top of the water but the majority of it in under the water far from sight. We had successfully kept on our mask for a few years. He was doing him and I was doing me! Life was rapidly changing as I continued with my career and education but I didn't particularly see how much it was changing.

My husband didn't have any biological children at the time that we got married. As a matter of fact, he had been convinced that he couldn't have children. God bless my pastor who told him that he would have children and that God just wanted to make the right connection so that his children would receive the covenant that was promised him. I wasn't convinced initially! I was 40 years old and had no intentions of starting this parenting thing over again.

My husband told me during our first year of marriage that God had promised him two sons. I was like Sarah, I laughed! Of course, I had no indication that it couldn't or wouldn't happen since we were fulfilling our marital vows regularly. Side note, but not a side note: we kept ourselves pure until our wedding night! When I found out shortly after my 41st birthday, that I was pregnant, I had mixed emotions! It was the joy of knowing that God had honored our marriage covenant that included being fruitful and multiplying. I told myself that maybe God did promise him a son! Okay, let's do this. But I was 41 years old ~ My daughter was almost 12! How was I going to be able to have a healthy baby at that age? I was also still in a stressful executive position on my job and had recently returned to school to work on my doctorate degree.

That all worked out fine and on September 30, daughter number 2 was born! I had a very healthy uneventful pregnancy. I was still thinking about what my husband said about God promising him two sons. I figured that they, he and God, had gotten it kind of wrong because he now has two daughters ~ right? WRONG? Nine months down the line, I could not figure out why my nursing milk was not producing the way it had in the past. Guess what, I was pregnant again! Eighteen months later, I had son #1. This pregnancy was a little different from the last. I was still working, going to school and holding things down at home and church. Number 1 son was super active in my belly which caused the doctors some concern especially at the age of 42; some of my prenatal test were also showing some abnormalities. He was born normal, healthy and fat ~ 8 pounds 3 ounces when I was 43 years old.

As you could quite imagine with two children under the age of two, at 43+ years old, working full time and trying to hold things down at home and church (I had taken a break from school), I was tired all the time. At this time, my husband was teaching private vocal lessons full time. He had opened a school in the other house that we owned and spent quite a bit time there. I felt like the weight of all of the responsibility was on my shoulders. I felt like I was doing everything while he got to do what he loved doing.

Bitterness and resentment started to build! Mind you, he had already hired a housekeeper to help with the heavy cleaning in the house. I can honestly say that we have never had a volatile relationship. Up until that time, three years in, we had never even had an argument. But I was tired! He was coming home later and later. The pressure was building in the pressure cooker and when he finally came home one night I let him have it. I told him how tired I was and how I couldn't carry all of this weight by myself and that I felt like he could be doing more to help me. He didn't raise his voice as he said, "I didn't think you needed me! You made what you do look so easy." He explained that was his reason for staying at the school so late every night because he felt like I didn't want or need him around. He felt the tension rising in our home but WE never took the time to address the rhino in the middle of the room.

We began to realize that we didn't communicate as well as we thought we did. It took us some time to get to the point of building strong communication because in the midst of this time period we discovered that there were many more things that we were keeping from each other. We had to dedicate ourselves to dealing with some hard truths. What helped us to really face the tough conversations is that we knew each other's heart and that we really genuinely loved each other. It didn't make conversations any easier but it made making amends better. Well, let's just say that over the next year or so, things got better and son #2 was born!

For Richer or For Poorer

As a successful career woman, as well as one that began

managing a household at a young age, I prided myself on being able to manage money well. Before getting married, I managed to take the money that I made and made sure that my bills were all paid on time. I didn't always have a lot left over but I always had a plan for how to make money stretch. The biggest secret to my success was that I began tithing to God at the age of 16 and with very few exceptions, never stopped. With the money that I kept after tithing, I still managed to pay my house note, car note and other regular bills, keep my daughter in private schools, take at least two vacations per year and help those in need. I have always been a giver. I love blessing people. There was rarely a time that I didn't see someone in need and didn't help them. That was just me.

When I got married, I relished the thought that now there were two of us and we could do twice as much. I knew going into marriage that I had the senior income in the household because my husband was a business owner primarily but also received a stipend from the church for the program operations and music ministry work that he did. Making more money than my husband didn't bother me because we were now one…so I thought. We were one in most aspects but had very different ideas about money. I believed in paying my bills on time, not carrying extraneous debt, and maintaining my 700+ credit score; he on the other hand didn't share the same value.

We talked about finances briefly in premarital counseling never really delved into the real state of affairs with his finances. I would later learn that he had a lot of outstanding debts and collection accounts that scared the heck out of me. We did not share the same values about how to pay bills. Every time I tried to talk about money and bills the entire mood of the house would change. At the time, I was writing the checks for all of the bills in the house. Little did I know that even though we had previously agreed to this, it was a bone of contention. We decided to switch it up. I gave him my checkbook (we didn't have a joint checking account at the time) and the bills and trusted him to pay the bills.

What happened next was more than I could handle. We began getting disconnection notices and late charges on bills; for the first time in my life one of my utilities got cut off. The money was there; I made sure of that so why were these things happening? What I didn't know was that his perception of paying bills and mine were totally different. My practice was to pay bills, the entire bill when it was due if not before; his practice was to pay on it whenever. Our vows were really tested because now we began to disagree more often because I was angry.

I'm the analytical mind in the family. I have to process everything! My husband is the more reserved, artistic one that don't always articulate. My need to discuss things became more like nagging to him until one day he yelled at me, "I'm not one of your employees. Stopped trying to administrate this house!!" My feelings were hurt and I shut down because I beat up on myself for not knowing these things in advance of being married but also because we were unable to communicate about them.

My husband had been self-employed and in full time ministry for many years. He had traveled all over the world in ministry as an international psalmist. He traveled with some very highly acclaimed ministry leaders and was sought after for the anointing on his voice. He had also owned a very popular barbeque restaurant on the Northside of Chicago that I had visited on several occasions when I visited my childhood friend that lived in that area. He had done parts in a couple of hit movies and been on sound tracks to several others. His claim to fame was also the hundreds of commercial jingles and voice overs that he became famous for. I said all of that to say that he was not a stranger to money; he was just not a good manager of money. I bluntly asked God in prayer one day, God why did his previous wives have the benefit of enjoying all of the money and I don't. The answer came back, he will have it again and you will be the one that will help him keep it.

During this time, the third part of our vows began to get tested. My husband began to suffer some the effects of being morbidly obese which caused him to have to close his school. Of course, this was now absent income. Unfortunately, we had fallen into the trap that so many other couple fell into of somewhat living above our means. We are not extravagant people however instead of us living off of one salary and saving the rest, we were spending it all paying bills and providing for the family. By this time, we were living in a very nice five bedroom, four bathroom house, we had a second house that had a mortgage, we had 3 vehicles, 4 children, and the list of responsibilities goes on. Doesn't seem like much but when the needs increase but the income is cut, it creates quite a crisis. The salary that used to support two people now had to support six (I didn't get raises back in those days because of my job title).

Devastation was abounding as our finances were crashing in on us. I again felt the weight of the world on my shoulders as my husband who didn't appear to care about money went on as though everything was fine. Here comes a moment of sadness and vulnerability as I share what happened over the course of the next year of this financial crisis. I didn't know that my husband had not been paying the mortgage on the second house that he was using as the school and was barely paying his car note. The house was foreclosed on and the car was repossessed. This was a defining moment in my life.

In Sickness and In Health

When we married, my husband and I lived very different health lifestyles. My daughter and I were vegetarians while he was a licensed chef. My daughter often joke about how we ate stir fry for seven years while being vegetarians although that was so not true although she was so grateful when he came along and began cooking for us. My husband was morbidly obese when we married. At the time, that didn't stop him from doing anything that he wanted to do.

Over the course of time, his body experienced structural problems that began to affect his mobility. He developed degenerative and bulging disc in his spine along with the degeneration of cartilage in his knees and hips. He had not and would not work toward losing the weight so the conditions continued to deteriorate. I never knew the affect that all of this would have on me and my children. His condition deteriorated so much that at one point he was using two canes to walk. His doctors continually suggested that he lose weight but he thought that they were just judging him based on his size. His doctor recommended to him that he consider a weight loss surgery but he would have no parts of it. He got mad and fired his doctor who was our family doctor that we really adored. The doctor's constant suggestions along with his deteriorating condition and lack of finances, sent him into somewhat of a depression. No one recognized it because he was still his upbeat gregarious self in public but at home, he moped around and was very moody. He was not really motivated to do anything but cook and eat and of course make love to me. Thank God, the love making has never suffered ~ sorry, I digress!

All while he went through this process, again more weight fell on me as I took on more responsibility in the house. The kids were young so they weren't able to do much to help. One morning during our talk time, he said to, "I'm going to have the surgery." It seemed like a random statement because it had been almost a year since we had even discussed this. I was thinking he was talking about having either hip or knee surgery because he was in constant pain. What I didn't know was that he had been told that he couldn't have hip or knee surgery until he lost weight. The surgery would not be effective with the weight that he carried. I said, "Which surgery?" To which he answered, "weight loss surgery." He had done an extensive amount of research over the year about the gastric bypass surgery and it helped him to alleviate the fear that he had about having surgery.

He later told me that he decided to conquer this fear because he had children that he wanted to be around to see grow up. Part of his depression stemmed from not being able to go out and play with his children or go to amusement parks with them. He rectified relations with our family doctor. He scheduled an appointment just to go in and repent to our doctor. The doctor didn't know that he had been angry or that he had started seeing another doctor. Once he made amends, our doctor bent over backwards to make sure that he had everything that he needed to be successful with every surgery. Favor became my husband's middle name!

In March of 2012, he had the first of which would be five major and one minor surgeries in two and a half years. 2012 proved to be a tough emotional year for us. Shortly after the gastric bypass surgery, my mother-in-love got mortally ill. She passed away in May of that year but before she died, she told him to make sure that he did whatever was necessary to take care of himself so that he would be around for his wife, children, and his sisters. That admonishment became the building block for him to start taking better care of himself. Additionally, that year, the hospital that I worked at 5 minutes away from home closed down forcing me to take a job downtown and then on the north side of Chicago. All of this while working on my dissertation to complete my doctorate degree! I was an emotional wreck most of the time although no one really knew it.

The testing of our vows was the making of me understanding my anointing for being married to Tony Powell. Despite my age, I found that I had to grow up really fast. I had to learn a new way of communicating with both my husband and with God.

His fault in our vows getting tested was that he fought through whatever it took to overcome the difficulties that he was facing to make sure that he was my perfect husband. My pastor used to always say that her husband was not a perfect man but he was her perfect husband. I now knew first-hand what she meant.

It Comes Down to Choices

We had a rough couple of years as we worked through learning who we were and how to be married to each other. It was never a matter of whether we would continue to be married but how to be married! Every time a rough patch came, I would remember the statement from premarital counseling, "I'm anointed to be married to him." Did it make the rough patches easy to go through, absolutely not but it did make me put my faith and trust in God to the test? I have seen so many people run for cover at the first sign of trouble. The cover that they run for is not the cover that can really help them. They run for the cover of a separation or a divorce court.

Remember in chapter one when I talked about how I used to pray for marriages and even sometimes counsel married women even before I got married. One of my advanced degrees is in Counseling and Guidance. Some of the things that I heard these women say gave me insight into how easy marriages fall apart. Some of those reasons stemmed from no premarital counseling to pure selfishness of the woman thinking that the marriage was supposed to be all about them, so they rushed to get married because they were having premarital sex. Rarely did I hear stories of biblical reasons for divorce i.e. infidelity or abuse. My approach was always to take them back to remembering what they loved about their spouse. I often gave homework to make two list: one list of all of the great things about their spouse and one with all of the things that they saw as challenges. I always reminded them of why they originally fell in love with them. Again, very rarely did I hear that they didn't love their spouse or that they never loved them.

The counseling experiences helped me to know that I was really in my marriage for better or for worse, for richer or for poorer, and in sickness and in health. My husband was (and is) an exceptional man! He was God's choice for me and I had decided that I would ALWAYS fight for my marriage. He was God's man first and foremost. I was convinced that God would not have prepared me over the ten years that I was not in a romantic relationship with anyone to have me be by myself again. During those years, that I was by myself, I had absolutely no idea how God was transforming my mind and my thinking to prepare me for the years ahead of me. I allowed God to make me new so that my husband could have a fresh new bride. I could have kicked against the pricks of what God was doing in my life because of course I had choices but I also had a daughter that I never wanted to compromise in relationships the way I had in times past.

During a time in my marriage when things felt the toughest, I cried out to God, "God, I didn't sign up for this!!" Before I could say another word of complaint, I heard the words, "Yes you did!" I stopped crying and began to remember my vows … for better or for worse, for richer or for poorer, in sickness and in health. Ruby E. Powell, you are anointed for this!

I also had the choice to treat my husband like the king that God made him to be. I remember early in my marriage, one of my friends started a support group for married women. I was one of the charter members of the group. As part of this group there was an early morning prayer call once a week. Week after week, the women would talk about concerns that they had in their marriage. Many of the concerns sounded so self-centered.

One morning, I was asked to share my success in marriage because I never seemed to complain. I shared two principles. One, I believe that my duty as a godly wife was to serve my husband and two to treat him as a king. There were gasp, groans, and sighs as I explained what I meant. I explained that I only gave out what I wanted to get back. If I treat my husband like a king, he will then treat me as his queen.

Give, and you will receive. Your gift will return to you in full—pressed down, shaken together to make room for more, running over, and poured into your lap. The amount you give will determine the amount you get back (Luke 6:38). So often people use this scripture to talk about giving of money and things. There is absolutely no mention of money in this scripture. Luke 6 is a book of instructions about how to treat people! Consequently, if I give my husband love, I will get back an abundance of love; if I serve my husband, I will receive an abundance of acts of service. There are so many things that my husband does for me as acts of service that are the result of my serving him and treating him as my king. I remembered how Sarah called Abraham Lord because he was her designated covering (I Peter 3:5-6). Abraham was not by any means perfect but God still called him righteous. My husband was not by any means perfect but he was my perfect husband because God called him righteous. He became the standard for our marriage.

I made the choice to make sure that my husband's name and character was always protected. Most people saw him as the international psalmist and minister, the jingle singer and voice over artist, the dynamic vocal coach, the chef, the movie star, etc. I saw him as my husband and king. As I made the choice to cover his frailties, I didn't have anyone that I could talk to about my hurts and feelings. I also remembered what my spiritual father said that day in premarital counseling, "I better not ever see her come in here crying because you mistreated or didn't honor her!" So again, I smiled and never let on that we were experiencing some of the things that we were. Through it all, I knew that I was never alone, because my spiritual mom was perceptive and wise. She never said a word to me but I knew that she was praying for me.

When Love Becomes a Who, Instead of A What

So many people have attempted to answer the question of what is love. Unbelievably with all of the marriages and weddings that take place very day most people get that answer terribly wrong!! Love is often described as an emotion or feeling. That feeling is often equated to butterflies in the stomach when that person is around or a swooning feeling that bring about a smile, giggle or laugh. The dictionary even describes love as a noun indicating a profoundly tender, passionate affection for another person; a feeling of warm personal attachment or deep affection, as for a parent, child, or friend; a sexual passion or desire. If that is the only way to describe it, I guess it will suffice but I beg to differ.

Growing up in Sunday school and church we always sang a song that says, "Jesus loves me this I know, for the Bible tells me so; little one to Him belong, they are weak but He is strong!" We always saw pictures of Jesus playing with children and showing tenderness toward children. Christians were described as children of God. To me Jesus has always been representative of love. It's not just because of those pictures but because of who He is. Those pictures always made me feel warm and fuzzy. So often in my life I had to picture myself as one of those children playing with Jesus and being loved by him! But Jesus said, "Let the children come to me. Don't stop them! For the Kingdom of Heaven belongs to those who are like these children." (Matthew 19:14). Jesus wanted to pray for them and impart His wisdom and knowledge that can only be found within the Kingdom of Heaven. Wow, what love would someone have for his children that he would want to give them the whole Kingdom of Heaven! Matthew 6:10b says, "May your will be done on earth, as it is in heaven." God wants Jesus' love that is displayed in heaven to be done on earth through us!

In the New Living Translation of the Bible, love is referenced 759 times. That's a whole lot of love. What makes the love of the Bible so astounding is that emotion is most often preceded or proceeded by an action. The dictionary also defines love as a verb but it still points back to self ~ to have love for or to have a profoundly tender affection or passion for. One of the most famous verses in the Bible say, "For so LOVED the world that He GAVE…" (John 3:16 KJV) need I say more. Throughout the new testament especially, when love is mentioned it talks about an act of giving or serving.

Love is sometimes a sacrifice. Sacrificing can be an extreme act of love as it causes one to give up something of high value in exchange for something that is of higher value. The issue is that the higher value is not always seen right away. I have always been a giver but there is nothing like when someone ask me to "save me a piece of that sandwich, or can I have that last piece of cake, etc."; my mouth was set for that last, little morsel. In times past, I would say, "let me just buy you one or make you one" but that is not really a sacrifice now is it!?! Anyone could do that but the one who LOVES make the sacrifice to adjust their appetite for the sake of another. Why do I go into this detailed discussion about love and how it's defined? What does it have to do with my marriage and it being all his fault? As I said earlier, the word love has been so misused that it has sometimes become valueless. It's easy to say, "I love you" when it doesn't cost you anything.

So many times, in my marriage, my husband made the sacrifices necessary to be to his family the person that God said he should be. He has beat himself up so often because he wanted to be a better provider or a better lover or a better giver or a better father or a better whatever! Sometimes him beating himself up came across as brash or abrasive to those around him however his desire to be better was much stronger than his desire to stay the same. Did he always do the things necessary to make himself better? Nope ~ not right away!! Did he always want to hear my subtle "encouragement" asking him did he do this or do that? Nope!! Did I always feel good about having to remind him to do things or taking the lead to do things? Nope but he sucked it up and moved forward toward the greater good for our family. You see, I learned to see my husband for who he is instead of who I wanted him to be. I could not make him a better man, that was God's job, I could only pray and remain in the role of the helpmeet!

When I wanted to nag instead of encourage, I had to see him. When I wanted to do instead of wait for him to do, I had to see him. When I wanted to be angry instead of be patient, I had to see him. He became my picture of love. He was the 'who' in my love! Don't get me wrong, I still wanted what I wanted when I wanted it but the love of God in him became my motivation to adjust my way of thinking and my way of doing things so that I didn't destroy the plan of God for his life. Jeremiah 29:11 is one of the reminders that we live by daily! As a matter of fact, we have a banner of that scripture hanging at the midpoint of our staircase so that it can be seen every time we come in the house and every time we go up the stairs. I have always been a take charge, get it done, get it finished type A personality. I want people to hold me accountable and thus I hold others accountable. Recognizing that everyone is not wired the same way helped me to see that God loved me so much that me put two seemingly incompatible people together and made us one!

His only fault in becoming my who instead of my what is loving God more than he loves me so that God could make him into the man that he is supposed to be!

Our Criteria Became the Word of God

Throughout any of the challenges that we have had, I never had any doubts about his love for me. We took the scripture in Genesis 2:24b serious as it said, …two shall become one flesh! When I hurt him, I'm also hurting myself because we are one! I've learned to love myself and have no desire to hurt myself! We have never been a couple that is prone to argue and fight ~ it takes way too much energy for that! At our age, we have to conserve energy for things that are more important. There were times that we had to have very strong discussions about things and we made a choice early on to disagree without becoming disagreeable.

This choice was made after we had our very first real argument. We were in our bedroom with the door closed but the argument became quite loud! Our little ones were about two, four, and five years old came and knocked on our bedroom door with arms locked together and tears in their eyes and said, "Mom, dad, are you all getting a divorce?" Woooeee, that was a stark and startling statement coming from children so young! First of all, what did they know about divorce at their young age and second of all, had we let our emotions get so out of control that it disrupted the peace and security of our home. We had always prided ourselves on maintaining a peaceful environment in our home despite the noise and chaos that a family of six would cause especially with three children so young. People would come to visit us and all of a sudden find themselves dozing off on the couch; they would wake up in amazement saying that the peacefulness of the home lulled them to rest and sleep. We looked at each other and decided that there is nothing so serious that the security of our children would ever be threatened at home again. I believe that scared us back into the reality of what God called our marriage to be. We were not only to be a sanctuary for each other but also for others that need to rest in their relationships.

From that moment on we became more conscientious of what the word said about our relationship. Our relationship was to be a standard for not just marital relationships but relationships of all kinds ~ parental relationships, sibling relationships, working relationships, friendship relationship! There is no relationship on earth that could not benefit from seeking the peace that we receive so freely as a gift. "I am leaving you with a gift—peace of mind and heart. And the peace I give is a gift the world cannot give. So, don't be troubled or afraid (John 14:27).

Our pastor taught us that peace means that there is nothing missing, nothing broken, nothing needed, nothing wanted, and nothing wasted! Does that mean that we have everything at our disposal? Of course, it does not! What it means is that in every state or condition that we are to be at peace and be content (Philippians 4:11). In all types of relationships, people find it hard to give up the "fight".

No one wants to be wrong or seem as though they have lost the fight. We fight for the right to be right! What's most important in relationship ~ the need to be right or the need to be righteous! We choose to be righteous because righteousness brings about peace. I decided that I would always do my part to be righteous so that the peace in our relationship is not disrupted.

There was a wife in our church that would always quote Proverbs 31:10-31. As I started listening to that scripture more carefully and what it was really saying;

Who can find a virtuous woman? for her price is far above rubies ~ rubies are more valuable than diamonds!

The heart of her husband doth safely trust in her, so that he shall have no need of spoil ~ her husband does not have to worry about her being wasteful!

She will do him good and not evil all the days of her life ~ she treats him like the King that he is in her life!

She seeketh wool, and flax, and worketh willingly with her hands ~ she is not concerned about breaking a finger nail!

She is like the merchants' ships; she bringeth her food from afar ~ she provides food for her family!

She riseth also while it is yet night, and giveth meat to her household, and a portion to her maidens ~ she is not a slackard!

She considereth a field, and buyeth it: with the fruit of her hands she planteth a vineyard ~ she is skilled in real estate!

She girdeth her loins with strength, and strengtheneth her arms ~ she takes good care of her body!

She perceiveth that her merchandise is good: her candle goeth not out by night ~ she works late if necessary!

She layeth her hands to the spindle, and her hands hold the distaff ~ she is a skilled homemaker!

She stretcheth out her hand to the poor; yea, she reacheth forth her hands to the needy ~ she is a giver!

She is not afraid of the snow for her household: for all her household are clothed with scarlet ~ she makes sure her family have warm clothes for the winter!

She maketh herself coverings of tapestry; her clothing is silk and purple ~ she is a makes her own clothes!

Her husband is known in the gates, when he sitteth among the elders of the land ~ she has high moral character!

She maketh fine linen, and selleth it; and delivereth girdles unto the merchant ~ she is an entrepreneur!

Strength and honour are her clothing; and she shall rejoice in time to come ~ she works keeps a good attitude!

She openeth her mouth with wisdom; and in her tongue is the law of kindness ~ she speaks words of wisdom!

She looketh well to the ways of her household, and eateth not the bread of idleness ~ she is in no wise lazy!

Her children arise up, and call her blessed; her husband also, and he praiseth her ~ her family recognize her hard work on their behalf!

Many daughters have done virtuously, but thou excellest them all ~ she operates in a spirit of excellence and sets a high standard!

Favour is deceitful, and beauty is vain: but a woman that feareth the Lord, she shall be praised ~ she is not so focused on outward appearance!

Give her of the fruit of her hands; and let her own works praise her in the gates ~ she does not have to brag on herself; just keep doing you girl! (Italics mine)

Until the true criteria for my marriage became the word of

God, I never really meditated on that scripture. This scripture has been the main scripture that has been used to describe wives. I had heard so many women vehemently say, "I'm a Proverbs 31 Woman!!" When I started meditating on this scripture, I started questioning if they truly knew what they were talking about!

The Proverbs 31 woman was no punk! She had at least nine job! O my God! Am I even half that woman! Some twenty first century woman will say, who's gonna do all of that!?! Others will say, what is he gonna do for me!?! It really does come down to choices!

The Proverbs 31 woman was not at all selfish. She took her roles very serious. A Godly man will recognize the sacrifice that she makes for him and the family. That's why he praises her and the children call her blessed! A Godly man will treat his wife like a queen because she is intentional about treating him like a king!

The Proverbs 31 woman was leading by example. She is teaching her children how to serve therefore they are the fruit of her hands and show appreciation for all that she does for them. The scripture does not indicate that the Proverbs 31 woman is subservient as some would say!

This scripture became the criteria for how I honored my husband and family. I see my children as a reflection of me; yes, it seems like a lot but I am happy to be that example for them. I want my husband to be looked at reverently for the man of God that he is! I promise you that I am no saint! I miss it miserably sometimes! I do get tired and I some days don't want to do anything but be lazy! Girl, give yourself a break!

What was his fault, he recognized my worth and value! He began to treat me more like a queen because of my stance to honor him as a king!

Our 4-B Principle for Life & Marriage

One of the things that we had to determine about our marriage is that we would never negatively blame each other for the things that have been challenges for us. We are a team and will never win if we are playing on different teams. I am the analyst in the family so I always have to have a plan; my husband is artistic so he believes that everything will work itself out. I am structured, he is flexible! How does this work as a team? Our differences could have been a breaking point for us but we decided that it was more important for us to utilize our individual strengths and build from there. At one point in my life, I was so rigid that if things didn't work the way I planned that it would send me into a tailspin. My husband, on the other hand, floated through life like, Que sera sera! Whatever will be, will be! What the heck!

My mindset was the result of being in a very self-imposed protective stance. I was always on the defensive waiting for the next person to hurt or disappoint me. I'm so thankful to God that I have reached a point in my life in which I have released my pride and I'm willing to admit that I was a for real mess! Through our 4-B Principle, I have allowed God to begin transforming my messes into a real masterpiece.

There was a time when I would never have talked about some of the challenges in our life ~ I certainly would not have put them in a book for the whole world to see! As I said in Chapter 6, my criterion is the word of God. Whenever I feel challenged by life and marriage, I look to the word to be a guide! Here is the standard that we use to guide our life and marriage.

Be Prayerful

Both my husband and I have studied the word of God extensively and both had strong prayer lives but there was something that was missing in our relationship ~ we didn't pray together for US! It was not that we never said a prayer together, it was that we didn't have a consistent prayer life together. We would intercede for others and we even prayed for each other but we didn't take the time to decide what our prayer needs were and spend time praying and speaking the word of God over our life together.

At one of the challenging times in our life, I was working on the far Northside of Chicago. At the time my husband and I were sharing a car because we had lost the other one. I typically would take public transportation to work because it was more convenient. One morning my husband decided that he wanted to drive me to work. It just happened to be one of those days that I just wasn't really feeling him so to be in the car with him for over an hour was going to take something on my part.

As we were driving along in silence, he said to me, "What do we need to pray about today?" I didn't quite understand what he was talking about because I had already had my prayer and devotion time for the day. Yes, I was still feeling some kind of way about him even after having been in the presence of God! Help me Lord! I answered, "Excuse me." I had totally missed the operative word, "We". He said, "One of the things that's missing in our life and marriage is that we don't pray together. Yes, we both pray. We both pray for each other but we don't pray together."

I had not ever really thought about that. He began to make driving me to work a ritual so that we could have our prayer time together. Each morning we would decide what we needed to pray about. Many of our prayers were prayers of intercession but the important thing was that we were in unity. It became important for us to take the time to decide what and who we need to pray for each day.

Our prayer time became a priority for us. We take pleasure in coming together to commune with God. Our communion time with God helped to create a different level of intimacy in our relationship. It does each of our hearts so much good to actually hear how we pray for one another's needs, desires, and concerns. It brings us joy to celebrate each other's victories when prayers are answered for us and for others. Through our prayer time, we realized how much we enjoyed spending time together. We get to be silly together, we get to laugh together, we get to cry together ~ our safe place is together! That together time leave little room for us to grow apart. Praying together helped to build the team spirit even more so as we prayed together with pure motives truly wanting God to answer our prayers.

Be Patient

Ever heard the term that Rome wasn't built in a day! Well a great marriage is not built in a day! It goes way beyond the wedding day! The wedding day is just the public witness of your covenant and commitment to one another. It is the day that everyone gets dressed up and show up to see how pretty the bride looks, how handsome the groom is, what the bridesmaid dresses will look like! The bride feels like a fairy tale princess and the groom meets her at the altar as the knight in shining armor! You make the vows, "for better or for worse, for richer or for poorer, in sickness and in health… till death do us part!" You leave the wedding and hopefully go on a honeymoon where you will consummate your marriage through making love for the first time as husband and wife!

What happens if things don't go quite as you planned! What happens if the "for worse" shows up shortly after returning from the honeymoon or even worse on the honeymoon! Fortunately, that wasn't our story but unfortunately, we lived with mask on for the first few years. We were still honeymooning and loving on each other! We were really living a charmed life! I was thanking God that waiting until I was 40 to get married paid off! I bragged about how we were having the time of our life during those first few years. I don't know what happened, but life showed up and the vows did get tested! I know I made it seem in the previous chapters that the tested vows were not that bad. They really weren't but any test can be trying when you're blindsided and the mask comes off unexpectedly. The truth of the matter is that the issues are always there but the bright light of goo-goo eyes and syrupy love don't let you see the signs! My encouragement is to do what the second 'B' of the 4-B Principle indicates ~ Be Patient!

If you know that God has put you together and that your marriage was truly made in heaven, don't fret! What God has put together let no one separate ~ not even you! There is no running away aka running home to mama and daddy! Patience is a virtue! It points you in the direction of righteousness and moral excellence. So, there is no cursing him out and telling him to get out of "your house". There is no doubting that God has done this! On your wedding day, two became one flesh so how prey tell do you separate from yourself. I know that I just got your blood boiling because some of you reading this are angry with your spouse or fiancé right now! Just like there are things about him that have started to get on your reserve nerves, there are also things about you that gets on his nerves as well. He's not a perfect man, you're not a perfect woman ~ but you are perfect together.

I talked in the last section about the importance of praying together but let me talk here about patience in prayer. As a seasoned prayer, I knew that I was off when I started praying selfish prayers of how I wanted God to change him. Every time I started praying, God make him do this, God make him do that, God change this or change that ~ well you guessed it! I saw absolutely positively NO CHANGES because my prayers were selfish!

After the frustration of praying ineffectively for a while, God pointed me to the scripture in Romans 5:2-4 KJV, "By whom also we have access by faith into this grace wherein we stand, and rejoice in hope of the glory of God. And not only so, but we glory in tribulations also: knowing that tribulation worketh patience; And patience, experience; and experience, hope:". The New Living Translation says it this way, We can rejoice, too, when we run into problems and trials, for we know that they help us develop endurance. And endurance develops strength of character, and character strengthens our confident hope of salvation (Romans 5:3-4). Well, you don't say! I began to appreciate the words that I said back in pre-marital counseling "I'm anointed to be married to him!" I quickly shifted my focus and began to say to God, "Father, I am grateful for the grace that you have given me to stand in the midst of tribulation. I thank you that the troubles are building patience and developing character in me."

It was no longer about Lord change him; it became about Lord, build patience and character in me as I hope for the salvation of my marriage! I had to wait on the Lord and be of good courage! I had to continue to treat my King like the King that he is until I began to see God work in my husband for God's pleasure! But if we look forward to something we don't yet have, we must wait patiently and confidently. And the Holy Spirit helps us in our weakness. (Romans 8:25-26a). Waiting patiently is not always easy but the reward of patience is so much greater than the anxiety of whining and bellyaching.

Be Proactive

Honestly, I think this is the best 'B' of the 4-B Principle! To be proactive is to get ahead of the game! If I had really listened when people said that the first few years of marriage are the most difficult, I would have been prepared for what eventually came. Don't get me wrong! I don't suggest that you are hypervigilant and looking for trouble around every corner but I do want you to be aware that two different people with different upbringing, different personalities, different DNA, bringing different sets of luggage from the past (yes, I did say luggage and not baggage), etc. create very unique dynamics in the marriage. I got to a point in which I was sitting back on my laurels saying, they were wrong, all wrong! We are good! We got this! I didn't prepare my spirit for what ultimately happened. So instead of praying for the grace to be the best wife that I could be I got comfortable and stopped praying for my marriage, for me and for my husband! Being proactive will prevent reaction when things begin to challenge the relationship! Reaction usually result in negative feelings, thoughts, and behavior. Being proactive allow you to initiate change instead of reacting to events. Reaction is like the gasoline of a smoldering ember; it causes a full-blown fire!

It is so vitally important to recognize where the potential flaws are in your own personality. That will prevent you from placing blame on your husband for things that he had no control over or no idea that they even existed. It took me a long time to realize that I had a real problem with communication. As talkative as I am, it took me being married to a real chilled dude to realize that talking is not necessarily communication. I didn't realize the importance of being able to communicate my needs and desires to my husband. I guess I just thought that he would magically know what makes me happy and what made me sad or angry. I blamed him for not knowing me.

As a trained counselor, I was violating the very rules that I would encourage in my clients. We often don't see the forest for the trees. We can help others identify their problem but not ourselves. More marriages (relationships in general) are destroyed due to ineffective communication. The day that my husband 'yelled' at me and told me to stop trying to administrate our house, I woke up to some startling realities that I was not communicating effectively. Communication can be difficult often because we take the risk to be vulnerable. If we have faced rejection in our life, we risk being rejected or thinking that our spouse will stop loving us because we spoke up. Because of the rejection that I suffered in relationships, both romantic relationships and friendships, I had instinctively decided that I wouldn't share my heartfelt feeling.

Premarital counseling is another way of being proactive. I'm not talking about the "Do you love him, do you love her, okay you can get married" type of premarital counseling. I'm talking about the counseling that examine every aspect of what you will encounter as a couple. We survived the tough times because we were able to go back to things that we discussed in premarital counseling and use the wisdom of our pastors to help us to open difficult doors.

We talked about everything from finances, to sex, to child rearing, blended family (I brought a daughter into the relationship), we talked about resolving conflict. Those discussions did not stop us from experiencing challenges but it gave us some tools to use when the challenges came. The Bible admonishes us that victory depends on having many advisers (Proverbs 24:6b NLT). Not just any advisers but those that are wise and have the best interest of your relationship at heart. It is never wise to talk to your single girlfriend that is angry because you got married and would love nothing more than to see you single again. Don't get counsel from your bitter divorced mother, auntie, or friend! Seek counsel from those that have overcome by the blood of Jesus and the testimony of those that have gone through the fire and came out without the smell of smoke!

Be Permanent

During the challenging times, it is easy to want to give up and throw in the towel! Don't do it! Remember the second 'B', be patient! Patience produces character and hope of salvation. No one ever said that marriage is not work. Not only is it work, but it can be hard work. On those days when you feel like calling it quits, remember your vows! This is when those words become more than just words said at a beautiful wedding ceremony. The wedding is just that day but the marriage is the … 'till death do us part!' That doesn't mean that you need to start plotting a murder ~ LBVS (laughing but very serious)!

It is the time to dig in your heels and make a declaration that the deadly 'D' word will never be a reality in your marriage. As I mentioned before, I remember clearly the day I said to God, "I didn't sign up for this" and He clapped back, "oh yes you did!" That was the first and only time I had ever said that. Even then I was in no wise considering leaving or divorcing or any such foolishness! I just wanted things to change so that we could go back to our happily ever after life.

Society have made divorce too easy. There are absolutely

biblical grounds for divorce such as adultery/infidelity but even with that, many couples have made the decision to stay together and overcome the violation that infidelity causes. I would never advocate for staying in an abusive marriage. That is not only physically dangerous but emotionally, mentally, and spiritually damaging. Apart from those two situations, the Bible does not support writs of divorce. Don't be afraid or ashamed to seek help when there are challenges that you two can't seem to figure out together. There are a multitude of Christian counselors that provide sound Godly wisdom that will help your marriage to remain permanent. Permanent means that your marriage will exist perpetually or for a long time without regard for unforeseeable circumstances (www.dictionary.com).

The 4-B Principle does not guarantee that your marriage will not experience some challenges or hardships but I'm certain that you will have some solid tools to refer to when those difficult times do come. You will learn to enjoy the intimacy of working through challenges together through prayer, communication, and selfless love.

This Story Closes, But the Journey Continues

When the blame game is done the right way, everyone wins. The husband wins, the wife wins, the children win, their entire circle of influence win! I look with anticipation every day to the rest of our life together. We have not ceased to have challenging situations. We have not ceased to have disappointing situations. We have not ceased to have lively discussions about things that we don't see eye to eye on but those lively discussions are always done as every day of our life is lived ~ applying the 4-B Principle. The story of how we overcame the rough times is over but our journey in life continues. I wake up every day knowing that Tony Powell is my priest, provider, protector, my lover, my best friend, my confidant, my baby daddy, the cream in my coffee and the apple butter on my toast.

We were recently asked to write a letter of encouragement to our spouse. It took me no time to compose my letter because I simply bore my heart regarding my King. I had to laugh at myself because when I got finished writing, I realized that I had been smiling the whole time I was writing. I want to share my letter with you in hopes that it will encourage you to write a letter of encouragement to your spouse. No matter how much we say I love you, we don't always take the time to tell them why we love them.

The letter of encouragement that I wrote to my King . . .

To My Priceless Perfect Husband,

Some would dare to say how could I call you my perfect husband when there are no perfect people ~ Well the operative word is MY perfect husband. God knew exactly what he was doing when he saved me for you. We had many chance encounters before he landed us in the right place at the right time to make a lifetime connection.

You lead our home with the love and care of God. You make sure that our children not only know who God is but have their own relationship with Him. I have watched you as you have grown in Him over these last 15 years of marriage. You have allowed God to help you to heal from church hurts that stemmed from childhood throughout your "church" life. This healing allowed you to go from religion to relationship with God! I recognize the effort, although it was sometimes painful but you always saw it as necessary.

We have had some really, really great times and we have had some challenging times. The challenging times were made perfect for us because we chose to go through them together. I don't take for granted all of the things that you sacrifice to make our family so much better!! My heart leaps for joy when you say that there is no place that you would rather be than at home with your family. I don't take for granted all of the things that you do to make my life easier and less stressful. It took me some time but I did learn the value of your heart ~ not that you do things the way I do them but your heart is to make sure that certain things I don't have to do like grocery shopping, cooking meals every day because you love to do it, doing laundry so that I don't have to, making sure the house is neat because you know that I like it that way, etc. Some of these things don't come natural for you but you love me enough to stretch yourself.

So, you may not be a perfect man but you are my perfect husband and I honor you every day and in every way! You still have so much land to possess ~ I know it because God promised it and He dare not lie!

I am honored to be selected to walk through life with you.

Precious
P ~n~ P Forever

By the way, P~n~P stands for Priceless (my nickname for him) and Precious (his nickname for me)!

If you are not at a point right now that you want to write the encouraging letter, I really do understand. Pull out a full-size piece of paper and divide it down the middle. On the left side of the paper begin to list all of the reason why you fell in love with your spouse. It may take some time. You may have to walk away from it and come back. Don't neglect to come back to the list; write until you can't think of not one more thing. On the right side of the paper, begin to write the things that are challenges in your relationship. Compare the two list! The person that you fell in love with is still there! He may be hiding behind hurt, insecurities, disappointments due to circumstances, or other things. Take the time to be prayerful, be patient, be proactive (it's not too late), and make the decision to be permanent. I would love to recommend a few resources to you (along with this book) that will bless your life and your marriage.

- The Power of a Praying Wife by Stormie O'Martian
- His Needs, Her Needs by Willard Harley
- Five Love Language by Gary Chapman
- 31 Days to Taming Your Tongue by Deborah Smith Pegues
- Reboot Your Marriage by Wesley and Neesha Stringfellow

Epilogue

It is always easier to blame another person for the things that happen in our lives. The blame usually leads to negative feelings, emotions, and behaviors toward the other person. Although Tony and I have had some rough times in our married life, we realized through the course of time that we are better together than we are apart. So why do we blame each other for being better than we were? We have learned to take responsibility for the perceived faults and failures that we have because of life experiences. No one can totally control the things that happen to them, but we can take responsibility for our reaction to them.

During those difficult times, we learned the art of communication and built a strategy for drawing back together instead of pulling away from each other. Please don't be disillusioned; we are still a work in progress, even at this point in our marriage, and expect that just as the scripture says, Jesus will keep working on us until he returns. I'm so grateful that we have allowed God to mature us through our experiences so that the blame game can be done to our benefit and not to our detriment. Our 4-B Principle works for us; it may not work for you, but I strongly encourage you all to develop a system that will be a go-to when times are difficult. Take the time to review and renew the covenant that you made with God and before your witnesses. There was a reason why you fell in love and made the commitment to each other—you are worth the work that it takes to stay together!

Ruby Powell

The voice of Dr. Ruby E. Powell has been heard as a corporate trainer, motivational speaker, and professional development consultant. Additionally, Ruby is a certified life/career coach, workshop leader, and curriculum developer. She uses her gift of teaching to motivate and encourage life change in people, both naturally and spiritually. Ruby is the Founder of the Oasis Empowerment Zone, Inc. (NFP), an organization that specializes in providing single mothers with encouragement and life empowerment through empowerment workshops, low to no cost (income based) life and business coaching, and networking opportunities with other single mothers.

Tony and Ruby are the parents of four dynamic children: Adya Monique, Kasiya Janae, Nathan Joseph Anthony, & Jonathan Christian. They along with their children have served in ministry for many years. They have all been bitten by the missions bug and look with anticipation to taking the gospel to every continent in the world!

It's All HIS Fault

It's *All* HER Fault

THE BLAME GAME
. . . THE RIGHT WAY

TONY POWELL

ITS ALL HIS/HER FAULT
The Blame Game The Right Way

Tony & Ruby Powell
tonyandruby@theblamegame.us
855-627-4748

Designed & Published by
PublishAffordably.com • 773.783.2981

Dedications

This book is dedicated to the memory of our spiritual mother, the late Apostle Jo Ann Long of *Let's Talk About Marriage and the Family* and to our spiritual father, Dr. John T. Long of *Adam Where Art Thou?* You all gave us a solid foundation for marriage and was dedicated to praying for our success.

To our natural parents, Porter C. Powell, the Late Elouise Powell (continue to rest in heaven), R.D. Roberson, and Mattie Williams. You all gave us life and taught us tenacity. Without tenacity, there are some days that we would have thrown in the towel. Thank you for always having our back.

To the Tribe of Powell (#TOPChronicles): our gifted, talented, and selfless children, Adya Monique, Kasiya Janae, Nathan Joseph Anthony, and Jonathan Christian. We can't thank you all enough for sacrificing so much of your time to allow us to minister to others; you recognize the value of what we are doing. We're thankful that God always make it up to you all!

To all of the relationships that will be helped as a result of our vulnerability and transparency.

Acknowledgements

We will not dare start to name all of our friends that encouraged us to write this book, you all know who you are!! We love you with all of our heart!

To our Pastors and friends, Jerry and Chris McQuay. Thank you for receiving us so lovingly into the family of Christian Life Center – Tinley Park and trusting us to serve as Elders in the church. We love you all tremendously!

To our writing team, Dr. Alice Maria Crawford, JoAnna Wilson, John and Deborah Anthony. Thank you for enduring the crunch time reading and solid feedback. To Marilyn Alexander ~ you have been telling us for the last several years that we had to get this done and held our feet to the fire until it was done!

Contents

Introduction

This book is a step by step account of how we met, married, and survived the challenges of marriage. We recognized how our upbringing and the examples of marriage that we witnessed formed unhealthy thoughts and marital behaviors.

Through good solid counseling and study of the Bible, we were able to develop a healthy respect for each other that formed a system for how to "place blame" in a more positive manner.

The 4-B Principle (Be Prayerful, Be Patient, Be Proactive, and Be Permanent) give detailed instruction on how to resolve conflict and create relationships that are enjoyable, productive, and fulfilling life.

It Started In Prayer, Literally

As a young man marriage was always something I looked forward to. I mean really, I loved the idea of marriage, so much so that my favorite childhood game to play in the house wasn't hide and go seek, it wasn't doctor—it was house. Now, it had its challenges of course. I mean, my sisters got tired of me making one of them be the mommy and the other one the baby, and neither one of them would let me run anything. That's right, no daddy rights!

Nevertheless, I looked forward to it, and this is why: in my early childhood, I saw a wonderful successful marriage between my mother and my father—at least so it seemed. It was almost storybook worthy. They were high school sweethearts, no other relationship before each other—yes first and only loves—they married as virgins, and they were devoted to God. They were devoted to their family, I mean gosh, it was like a black version of Leave it to Beaver!. They seemed to love each other so much, and I just wanted to have what I thought I saw they had.

But as good parents do, they protected their kids. They only allowed me to see the good side of things, and I didn't see

the difficult challenges they were really going through. So in July 1969, I experienced the shock of my twelve-year-old life. I was told by my mother and father, my perfect picture of life and family, that they were going to divorce. I saw that wonderful picture of marriage explode before my eyes, and the shrapnel from the explosion cut me in places I didn't know existed. It devastated me so much, my mother later told me that for six days, I spoke maybe 50 words, and those were in response to questions asked or directives received.

Within one year's time, I gained 65 pounds due to food binging and went into a depression that caused me to repeat a grade. I would eventually require mental counseling. Within the next three years, I would be put out of school, not once, but twice. I became a Black P-stone gang lieutenant, I stole my own godfather's 22-caliber revolver, used the city El train for target practice, smoked a dime bag every three days, and all this is before my 17th birthday! I grew up barely surviving my teen and young adult years. Look, my picture of the perfect life was already destroyed, and the worst part was my mental battle with the possibility that my parents' divorce might have been my fault.

It wasn't bad enough that my mom and dad no longer loved each other, but when they sat us down to tell us they weren't going to live in the same house anymore, my father looked at me and said, "So which one of us do you want to live with, your mother or me?" OMG! I was 12 years old, and they wanted me to answer that question! Well, I loved both my parents, but I was, and still am, a momma's boy. So as the process continued and the divorce became final, I had to deal with my father's demonstrated disappointment that I didn't

choose to live with him.

You see, my sisters and I were very close. They are both albinos, and I spent their childhood lives protecting them from all of the other kids' ignorance. My dad knew that as much as they loved him, the girls were going to go wherever I went. If he didn't get me, he didn't get any of his kids. That decision cost me a very painful adolescence; my dad became brutal concerning me. But that wasn't the end. My mother's pain, her midnight tears, and even her intense anger because he was gone—and with another woman at that—also cost me. Real pain, real hurt, must find a way of escape if we're ever going to heal. Unfortunately for me, I look just like my father, and sometimes I was the recipient of her anger with him. I didn't understand it then, but my mother and her therapist agreed it was happening.

My saving grace was that my mother was still a praying woman, and I learned, with help from her and some other God-sent people, how to pray as well. I finally became genuinely acquainted with God's salvation, and after some years of healing and grace, I became a new man with a new agenda. Outside of becoming a good Christian man and a fairly decent musician, I was dedicated and committed to having a marriage that worked—that would not fail. I was determined that I would not have the same type of marriage that my father had. I watched him not only betray and hurt my mom, but then marry and do the same thing again and then marry and divorce yet again. That's right, three times he failed (remember that number).

After watching and experiencing the pain that this had caused

everybody, even my two younger sisters, I vowed that I was going to have a successful marriage, and I really thought I was going about it in a realistic and even unselfish way. I swore to myself and to God that no matter what the challenge, I wouldn't quit; I would not get divorced. I even added this extra, self-righteous bonus. You see, the guys my sisters were in relationships with treated them very badly. They made bad decisions as young girls and had children out of wedlock. They were not given good examples of what they should have in a relationship from their father and, truthfully speaking, not from me either. They were treated like second-class citizens, and their "baby-daddies" were nowhere to be found.

So I made a commitment not only to marry and to sustain my marriage but to marry into a situation to hopefully help some young lady who had a child. Now I did have a bit of a criteria, which was that the baby's daddy could not be around, but other than that, it was my intention to hopefully be a blessing to both some woman and her child by marrying them and loving them the way God loves me.

Well, in June 1983, I did just that. I married a beautiful Christian young lady who had one child, a daughter and no baby-daddy; I was on my way, my dream was happening, just as I'd planned it, right? Wrong! My dream marriage turned into a nightmare, and I did not live on Elm Street. It was great for two years, challenging for the next five years, very shaky for the next four years, and the Twilight Zone for the final one. In total, it lasted for 12 years before it completely collapsed and fell apart. Within six months, I was divorced.

Now, I would love to put all of the blame in the other

direction; I would love to say it was the devil and her. I mean, don't get me wrong now, it was the Devil, and yes it was her—honestly a whole lot of her—but just as there are at least two sides to every story, some of this failure falls in my direction. I failed because I did not understand the workings of marriage as a young man. I had a picture of what I wanted marriage to be, but not a video—a snapshot, but not a "full feature" film. This is what I mean; a snapshot gives us a visual to aspire to, but there is not a plan on how to get there. You think that it means you commit to be faithful and to provide and to love, but it's sometimes—no, it's always—so much bigger than that. Especially depending on what type of baggage you bring with you to the marriage and what type of baggage they bring to the marriage and what kind of problems existed before you both came along.

Needless to say, the issues in everybody's lives are different, and the circumstances are different as well. We eventually ended up facing walls that other circumstances built that we could not work through together, and eventually it worked us apart. I ended up divorced, and my marriage promise to God and to myself was broken. I felt like such a failure that I decided I would not marry again…only to find myself married again. Now, in all fairness, the setup and scene for this one is different. I'd moved to central Illinois. I was in a new town, a different environment, working with a new ministry, but hauling the same relational baggage that I'd had in the previous marriage.

You guessed it, another woman, with another child, in another area, in another situation, and yes, another failure. The only thing that I seemingly learned from this marriage was how

to get divorced much faster. The first marriage lasted 12 years; this one lasted 12 months. I mean, try and wrap your mind around this: my personal marriage desire checklist stayed consistent. In both marriages, both were Christian women, both with only one child, both with the baby's daddy not in the picture. Yet the divorces had no commonality at all—I mean none! One woman was an introvert, the other was an extrovert; one was overly passive, the other overly aggressive; one child an angry 11-year-old girl, the other a 13-year-old emotionally wounded boy; one woman was not very clean and I'm being polite, the other was OCD on steroids!

After doing this a couple of times, I said to myself, "SELF" and myself said Huh, I convinced myself that it wasn't them, it was me! I was nuts to think I could do marriage. I mean look at my history. And here's keeping it real: the first marriage was done after much thought and logic applied. What did it get me? A big fat zero! Now the second time the problem was that instead of using my brain to think things out rationally, I used the "other" head. Nuf said. Nope, this marriage thing wasn't for me. I quit.

So, I came out of two badly broken marriages, hurting, wounded, and causing pain and difficulty in the lives of others. Someone very influential in my life taught me that "hurting people hurt people. My family and some friends felt my pain, whether they wanted to or not. I think the most painful thing wasn't the failed marriages but that, after all of that pain, I never lost the desire to share love and to be loved and to be a part of marriage as a Godly man and not fail, but be successful.

I left Central Illinois and came back to Chicago to hopefully start over again by myself. I joined a wonderful ministry called New Covenant Life Church, pastored by a wonderful woman, Pastor Jo Ann Long, who would eventually prove to be God's angel sent to me. She was the person who saw my bleeding, wounded heart after my marriages failed. She was the one who told me that "hurting people hurt people." You see, I told you, that although I loved my father, I was a momma's boy. Now, I can hear you whispering, "He's just weak." Not! I told you earlier: I was an officer under Jeff Fort, in the Stones.

I once, under the direction of my leader, instituted spin-roulette with a snub-nosed 38, point blank with a man's head. I pulled the trigger three times, upon command, while eating a Maxwell street polish & fries from Sammy's restaurant in Cabrini Green. I promise you that BC, that's before-Christ for those of you who aren't theologians, I was ruthless. I'm a singer and a musician by gifting. That makes me an artist, and yes, most artists are very passionate; it's one of the tools of the trade.

Passion is often fueled by nurturing, which is what mothers are primarily designed to do. In the course of my two marriages, I worked closely with five different pastors. Remember, I worked almost exclusively in full-time ministry, starting seven months after my first marriage. Of these five, Pastor Jo Ann Long was the fifth. All of the others were wonderful men of God. They gave me advice, gave me insight, gave me assignments, and prayed for me. She was the only one who gave me compassion and then nurtured me to wellness. I personally believe she helped save my life, and as

you will see in the next chapters, she did it in more ways than one.

Well, after becoming an intricate part of her ministry, I soon found out that this great woman of God was a specialist in marriage and family. I ended up becoming the chief engineer for a radio show that she hosted, entitled, "Let's Talk about Love, Marriage and the Family." You mean that there is someone actually helping marriages and family? On Monday through Friday, she would, for four hours a day, give counseling via the radio to people calling in seeking help and or answers. And wouldn't you know it, I, as her engineer, sat under this phenomenal teaching five days a week. Trust me, if you sit under somebody smart long enough, you just might learn something. All of the stuff I thought I knew about marriage, relationships, being a God man, I see now, I really knew very little. I said, "Wow, with the wisdom she has concerning relationships, every aspect of life should be good to go."

I've found this out about life: I may have plans, and we all do, but eventually my plans are going to run into God's will, and the determination is up to me as to whether or not I'm going to go with His will or my plans. That's why we call this the blame game the right way. You see, I've been married twice and I've been divorced twice. I could point out a lot of things that they did wrong, but if I'm really going to not just get better, but grow bigger, I'm going have to point out what I did wrong.

The blame, or the buck, as they say, stops here, no matter where it started. If we stop putting the blame outward and start looking to correct what is happening in us, find out

what I didn't do to produce the type of marriage that I so desired and actually take ownership of it, eventually, we will find the truth, and that truth will make us free.

I didn't have a good blueprint for marriage, so I had to use the sketches, pictures, and images in my head. Here is the reality: all of those things are subject to opinion and interpretation, but blueprints are not; they are exact in every way. They leave no room for error or opinion. Why? Because you're building something. When we allow God, He will show us the blueprint He has for our lives. Yes, God tells us clearly, "I know the plans I have for your life, they are good, and not bad in any way, to bring you a wonderful future filled with hope and expectation."

My entire world changed, and I'm putting this blame where it belongs: Pastor Jo Ann Long. You see, I now had a pastor and a teacher who not only loved me, but willingly nurtured me back to emotional health and taught me what was missing, the links that were not there for a good marriage, and then challenged me to say, "It's not over yet. I know what your plans say, but God's plan says otherwise." So the late Pastor Jo Ann Long, it was your fault.

As I said, I spent several years working with Pastor Jo Ann Long as the chief engineer for her radio show. Sitting in a studio listening to a master of marriage and relationships counsel people day in and day out is quite fascinating. For example, I learned that men fix stuff and women feel stuff. I learned that men just want to do it, whatever "it" is, and women want to discuss how they feel about doing "it." I learned that men really don't believe that the words "sex" and

"no" should ever be in a sentence together, that for women, size really does matter, and yes both men and women cry. All joking aside, I learned not so much about marriage, but really more about myself.

Over a period of four years, Monday through Friday, for four hours a day, I listened to her help people understand why their marriages were failing or hurting or trying to recover or missing something. The more I listened, the more I found help for myself. Yes, I finally had to look at me. I couldn't look at what the other person was doing wrong or right. I couldn't continue to blame situations, circumstances, and conditions as to why my marriages failed. I had to face the reality that there were some things I just didn't know, so therefore I couldn't do it right.

The other thing that I learned was that not knowing, in most cases, wasn't an indication of not caring. I didn't know better because if I knew better, I would've done better. The other thing that we have to face is that sometimes we don't really want to do better. What we really want is our way. I know in some areas I wanted it my way. I wanted my story to go the way that I'd envisioned it for my life, but God said he is the Author and the Finisher of this life and our faith. Through these years of assisting and serving Pastor JoAnn Long, I found that it was doing more than just helping me get through time. It was helping me to heal. The crazy thing is that I didn't realize how much I needed to be healed, and I realized that some of the healing that needed to take place could not take place because of all baggage I had carried from two previous marriages, as well as a ton of mistakes.

I guess it's good that God really is the Author and the Finisher of our lives. You see, I'd already determined that two divorces was enough. I would not get married again, ever. But one day, Pastor Long asked me, "What about children? What about family? What about legacy?" I actually responded, "What about it?" It's obvious it wasn't intended for me.

She didn't go along with my reply. I'd said it angrily, and she told me to check that attitude at the door! Well, I didn't want to go along with what she was saying either, so we were at an impasse. She was convinced that I would get married again. Yes, for a third time. My response was a laugh and a "God bless your ministry." Yes, pure sarcasm.

I had no intentions of marrying anyone. I didn't care how gorgeous, brilliant, or spiritual, my answer was the same: No. And keeping it 100% real, it was "Hell No!" I found out real fast that God really is the Author and the Finisher of our lives, and I want you to pay special attention to that word finisher for a minute.

Back in 1997, I had the privilege of being in a movie that was called Hoodlum, with Andy Garcia and Laurence Fishbourne. While on the set of that movie, I noticed three people always seated together on the set. They were sitting in little set chairs, and on the back of one chair it said, "Writer." This of course, was the writer of the screenplay, but directly to the side of that person were two other people. On the back of their chairs, I saw the strangest word. It was the word: "Finisher." I didn't tie it together at that time, but in asking Fishbourne who those people were, it was explained to me that Finishers were there because a director is responsible

for turning a screenplay into a motion picture.

Because of that, he has the right to change any scene in a movie that he or she so desires not to be there. They may feel it doesn't fit. They may feel it's not appropriate. They may want a total change in direction, and they're given that liberty because they have the overall scope of the movie. So the finisher's job is to tie together with the author and rewrite the script on the spot so that the story ends the way that it should, no matter what was taken out in the middle.

My screenplay for marriage, was good, but based on the co-star and supporting cast, the director couldn't make this movie work, in part, based on my mistakes, based on what I didn't want to go through anymore, I called it a wrap. But God, who was the author and the finisher, determined otherwise. Six months later, I started supervising an early morning prayer meeting at my church. A number of women would gather together in the mornings to pray. My job was to open the doors to the church, make sure that they were safe, accommodate them if they needed anything, and then lock up when they were done. One morning, while sitting in the office waiting for them to finish praying, this young lady came to the door who I'd seen before. She asked if she could use the phone for a minute; she needed to take care of something. I said, "Sure. Not a problem." I let her in the office, and I actually stepped out so she used the phone.

After I stepped out of the office, the strangest thing hit me. I thought to myself, YOU should ask this woman out for a date. Now of course the first thing I did was rebuke it because I knew it was the Devil himself, but afterwards I kept feeling

I should. Now I knew a little about this young lady. I knew that she was faithful to the church. I knew that she was close to my pastor, and I knew she had the most adorable little daughter. That was about all I knew about her, so I ignored it like any good twice-divorced brother would do and pushed the idea out of my mind. A week later it shot up again, so I looked at her one day, while she was passing the office. I said, "Excuse me please, may I ask you a question? If I were ever to ask you out for dinner or something, would you consider going out with me?"

She looked at me as if I had just spoken in a foreign language and said, "Well, yeah, I guess so." We both smiled, and that was the end of that. Within three months we went out on a casual date, including her precious little daughter. We had a great time, and sure enough, a real relationship blossomed. Within six months, I knew this woman was going to be my wife—you know, the wife I didn't want, a marriage I didn't want, but I knew she was the one. So I did what any red-blooded, chest-pounding man would do; I went into absolute denial! The next time I went into the radio studio, my Momma JoAnn Long, out of the blue, asked me, "Well Powell, what do think about this marriage thing?"

I looked at her and said, "Interesting you would ask me that because I believe I've met somebody who is supposed to be my wife."

My pastor actually put the radio show on autopilot. She turned herself off live air and said, "What did you say to me, son?" I repeated myself, and we proceeded to talk for about seven minutes until they called us from WYCA radio to ask

if we were having transmission problems. We went back on live and finished. When the show was over, she asked me, "Well, who do you think it is?"

I told her, "Ruby Roberson."

She said, "Ruby Roberson…my Ruby? Why Ruby? Is it because she's pretty and got big hips?"

I laughed and said, "My God! She sure does, but that's not the reason." I told her God told me she was the one, while she was in prayer and I wasn't even looking, for her or anybody. Pastor JoAnn Long then reminded me, "You said you weren't getting married no more." I said, "You're right Mom, but you said I would, and it looks like, as usual, you are right."

She then told me that she gave me permission and blessings to pursue this relationship. Within eight months, on the Sunday before Christmas 2002, I got down on one knee in my church before my entire congregation and asked this woman to marry me. And she said yes. I was in the right place at the right time. I was open to be corrected, to be healed, and to even allow the Author and Finisher of my faith to rewrite another chapter in my life. Needless to say, I had no idea that this third time really was the charm—that this time it was going to be not only right, but righteous— and best thing that ever happened to me. Not only that, she helped me find the right young woman, a Godly woman, an intelligent woman, a beautiful woman, an incredible mother who opens herself up to become that blueprint that God has for her life and mine. She was willing to go with the script.

Even though she knew I had baggage—yes, real heavy baggage—this incredible woman, who inevitably become my wife, said, "I believe I'm anointed to do this," and that was her Yes decision. I blame her for being courageous enough to take on the challenge of God when He said, "I've anointed you for this man." Are you willing to take the challenge? So Ruby Powell, I blame you totally for this, and because I blamed the right people, the best person, the chosen person, my world changed for the better, forever.

The Journey Together Begins

On May 31, 2003, my world and my life changed forever. I married the most incredible woman that I had ever met. We had a beautiful, incredible wedding. It was literally almost exactly like the wedding that Eddie Murphy had in "Coming to America." We had dancers. We had royalty. We had African garb. My daughter to be was dressed as our little princess. It was an incredible wedding. Our church was filled from front to back. We had at least eight hundred people in attendance. And not one, but two receptions. Needless to say, the man who had gotten it wrong twice finally got it right. I blame Jesus Christ for that. He was gracious enough to give me another opportunity and another chance at marriage. You see, we all "fall," but He, my Heavenly Father, didn't want me to fail.

I didn't realize then that he wasn't just doing that for me, but he was doing that for my heritage. He was doing that for people I would be connected to down the road, helping to teach and instruct them in the ways of God and marriage.

It was an awesome time, and it was an awesome new beginning. We had a wonderful honeymoon, and within the next year,

something I thought would never happen in my life happened. In my previous two marriages, I'd had no natural children. I was actually told by doctors that I might not ever have children because, number one, I was a very big man physically. I weighed over 500 pounds at one time, and I was told that because of my size, my internal body temperature in association with sperm activity could be reduced and that I may not be able to have children. I didn't think I deserved children anyway, especially with my marital record. But again, Momma Long said, "I believe God has a heritage and a legacy for you." Within the first year of our marriage, my queen became pregnant, and I became a natural birth father for the first time ever!

Wow, this really was surreal to me because it was a day I thought I would never see. Because I had no natural brothers, only sisters, I was the end of my line as far as our family name was concerned. Well, 18 months after that, we had another child, and 18 months after that we had another. We developed a wonderful relationship, and we grew together in so many ways, but needless to say, the richness of marriage and the richness of family does not mean that you continue straight through without any glitches or challenges.

Anyone who's ever been married or been in a real relationship knows that you go through many periods where you wonder, "Who is this person? Where did they come from? Is there a planet in the solar system that I didn't know existed?" And I assure you; they're thinking the same thing about you. But this time it was different because instead of pointing fingers and blaming, we were so busy looking at each other through the eyes of love and through the eyes of God, and we were

busy trying to find out what we could do to make this thing better. Whatever challenges came, we were willing to take them on together and to battle through them. Now I'm talking like this came very easy to me—it did not. In fact, I still, to this day, feel that too much talk is just unnecessary. You see, my idea of solid conversation and discussion was, "I don't think so, you can do it then, I'm right, then that settles it, how about a little bit" and that was enough. And to think, I was puzzled as to why I wasn't getting a little bit! In marriage, you're going to have challenges. You're going to have problems, but you can work right through them and make things better.

The third time really was the charm for me. Marriage has been a wonderful time of reconnecting with the truth of what marriage really is supposed to be about. I'm so grateful that I can blame this all on the Spirit of God and my wife because it opened up a whole new world to me, but that world was not a fairy tale world. There's a reality that is true in every situation when it comes to relationships, especially if it isn't your very first rodeo. You find out that whomever you meet, whatever love you find, whatever connection you make, you never come alone. You bring along an unwanted guest. It's called baggage.

3

What's Really In You Will Come Out!

Well, after a few years in, I've got a new wife, a new and growing family, new endeavors together, new horizons to enjoy. No, I kid you not, this time, marriage looked like it was going to be absolutely wonderful! My wife, yes the apple of my eye, was simply divine. And it was so refreshingly different. In my previous marriages, my choice of physical preference was short, about 5 ft, and petite. Neither of them weighed more than 175 lbs, with light cocoa complexions: you know, eye candy. Unfortunately, the outside was not a portrait of the inside. It ended up where one of them had almost no brains at all, and the other one had two brains! I'm serious; one was "slim-slow" the other one had dual personality disorder.

Trying to talk to them about serious things was like talking to Rainwoman or Dr. Jekyll & Mrs. Hyde. Now, I'm talking about them, but what does it say about me? Obviously, I'm no super catch either; at 6'2" in height and 468lb, they use to call me six-by-five. Why you ask? because I was 6 feet tall and 5 feet around. By the time we were beyond repair, both they and I realized that what we were experiencing with each other was always there, we just chose not to see it. Stuff from

their past, their upbringing, their hurts, their abuses, all found their way out, and I was the recipient of the past garbage they hid, under some pretty eyes, some luscious lips, some petite hips, and some sugary talk. I nicknamed it the marriage "rope-a-dope," and I'll give you only one guess who the dope was. But now I'm like Shug Avery from The Color Purple: "I's Married Now, again!"

My queen is 5'4", she's fine, she isn't petite, but surely "packaged," she a genius, she's got two masters degrees, she already owns a house and a car, she makes six figures a year, she loves God with all of her heart, and I'd hear music in the bedroom and there was no CDs playing, OMG! It was almost too good to be true, like a movie or something.

I'm not sure why, but it seems that in every good movie, there's a part that comes out of left field somewhere that is either dangerous or devastating. It will either scare the crap out of you, tick you off royally or have you in the "ugly cry" mode. Now, I'm one of those "need to know why" kind of people, so I asked a Hollywood director and friend, Bill Duke, "Why do y'all do that?" His reply was that it helps keep the person in their seat until the end, to see how it either gets better or gets fixed. And it also helps the person to better appreciate the climatic ending of the film.

It's called the past. Everybody has one, and every past is different. In most cases, there are some good things, but there's also some grief. We bring the pain and ugly side of our past with us because, most of the time, we don't want anyone to know about the "uglies" of our lives. One thing is for certain; you can try to hide it, but only for so long. You

can try to bury it. You can try to pretend it's not there, but eventually you will see that if you do not speak of your past, your past will speak of you. Your past will come out, by force if necessary, and in most cases, it comes out pretty ugly. Once that happens, any and everyone close to you will be affected, especially your spouse. That's when you find out that this wonderful thing called marriage has vows for a reason.

It didn't stop at "Dearly beloved." It didn't stop at, "Do you take?" In fact, It goes on to bring up real and very honest questions that require definitive answers. But do we really mean it? I found out that inevitably my past two marriages brought about not only some ugly baggage from my past but some real truths about myself as well. One thing you find out is that yes, your past may identify mistakes that were made, but it will also show you the errors of your own ways, and we don't like to deal with our ways. We can point fingers at that other person until the cows come home, but at the end of the day; we've got to be responsible for the baggage we bring. Those things we messed up from the floor up. Guess what, it's coming to the point where our vows are going to be tested, and those vows I made I didn't just make to my wife. I made those vows to God.

The truth of the matter is that when you enter into a relationship, you come in with smiles, hugs, and kisses, and yes, you bring baggage. Some good stuff, some bad stuff, stuff you're proud of, stuff you're ashamed of, but inevitably one day it's going to happen, and I promise you, when your past speaks, it doesn't shut up; it tells everything. One thing is for sure, when those bad habits come forward or those false expectations that you have get forced into the issue, this will

happen. The mask will have to come off.

I was and still am a control operator. I am the 'H.H.I.C.!' That is Head Husband In Charge! I'm the guy who doesn't speak much, but when I do, I'm right and it's law! I'm not always right, but I'm never wrong.

We try to put on this face that things are great, all the time—that we are always in a good place and that we have only good intentions and that everything is just perfect. But the truth is that we were masked. We put masks on to hide the frowns, the shame, the disappointment, the pain. In my case, it was two different marriages, both of which collapsed and failed miserably.

After being married twice, and failing the process, I felt loss was my just reward. I didn't have the children that I thought I was going to have. I lost property, l lost money, I lost prestige, I lost friends, I lost ministry, I lost…well let's just cut to the chase: I lost everything but my life. But there I was in a new relationship, hopefully to gain a new life, a new future, a new hope, and a new beginning. God says, "I'll give you those desires if you keep your hearts and minds on me. But you have to keep it real and you must take the mask off. You may even have to take the gloves off, too!"

Now, when I say take the gloves off, I don't mean we're going to blows, but guess what? We are not just people with faces; we're people with hands as well, and I had dirty ones, I didn't have a problem with stretching the truth if it served me, I didn't have a problem with employing manipulation if it served me. And serving me usually meant covering me.

The Bible tells us that we are not fighting flesh and blood, but we are in a fight. Sometimes our hands are cut and bruised and need healing. Sometimes those hands have the ugly dirt of the past on them. Sometimes they're scarred and have hard tissue on them and calluses from being abused as a child or being neglected as a youth or being told you'll never make it. Those hands are covered up with gloves—and sometimes with gloves that look just like regular hands that make them look nice and pretty.

But the truth is, we have to get naked before God; that's right, take it all off. Just like Adam and Eve were naked in the garden. They didn't think about clothing until they started acting a fool. They did not think about clothing until they disobeyed God and sin came in and the dishonesty came in and the knowledge of good and evil came into play. We have to take the mask off, and here's one of the reasons why. When you get married to that right one, not just that special one, the mask does something you do not expect; it becomes transparent. I was an ordained minister, with excellent music skills. I had been a professional singer and musician for several years—I mean a real professional, with W4s to prove it.

From 1985 until 2005, I sang jingles and did studio work with several national advertisers, to include Leo Burnett and Burrell International. I'd work with legendary producers and performers. I'd sang in international ministry circles with such notables as Oral Roberts, Kenneth Hagin, TD Jakes, and John Osteen (Joel was working in the church mailroom then). I'd been in major motion pictures and sung in 47 US cities and 11 nations of the world. Yet, with this resume, I was hiding my personal failures and inadequacies from

everyone I could, especially my wife. We cannot come into a real relationship and not allow that person to look us square in the eye and see us for who and what we are. Even if who we are doesn't line up or meet up to the standards of what we've done.

Now, let's deal with that: who we are and what we are. These are two different things altogether. Back in the day, when I did theological studies, one of my professors made this observation, and I found it to be true: if you ask 10 people, "Who are you?" seven of them will respond by telling what they do. You'll hear, "I'm a social worker," "I'm a detective," or "I'm an oral hygienist." What we do has importance, but it doesn't hold a candle to the incredible reality of who we are. When I asked him about his statement, he said, with great somberness, "Tony, some people live their entire lives never finding out who they are." I asked him, why does that disappoint you so? He responded, and I've never forgotten it, he said, "What you do can render success, but only finding out who you are will tell you why you're here and render fulfillment.

True story, I'm on my way back from a missions trip in 1991 from India. It was the worst/best missions trip of my life. Fifteen days in some of the worst conditions you could imagine: First, it was 27 hours in the air. Second, at 1:30 am, it was 97 degrees in Bombay. Third, they lost my luggage and it went to Paris, so I had no change of clothes in November; I left Chicago in black corduroys and a turtleneck. Remember, it was 97 degrees and the sun was not up yet! By noon the next day, the temperature hit 112 degrees, I am 6 ft 2 inches tall and weigh 325lbs. Nobody in all of India had

clothes to fit me. So I burned up for 3 days, in the same clothes. It got worse, but I'll spare you the details and summarize this way: I saw God, and I saw the devil, both up close and personal. On the plane heading back to the US, I was so happy to be leaving hell, I was singing on the plane, writing my own happy songs. My head was filled with music—then it suddenly stopped. God's Spirit spoke to me and said, "Get out your pencil and write." So I did. This is what God said to me, in an audible voice: "I have created you a Psalmist and a teacher, and the work that I've created you to do will take you outside of the four walls of the Church, to reach many." From that moment on, I've never had an identity crisis again. I know who I am, even if what I've done has changed, succeeded, or failed.

Now, this does not negate the fact that we are creatures of our environment. We are people with a culture. We are citizens with a heritage. We simply come together the way we were brought into this world. We all have those characteristics. I was deceitful because my daddy was deceitful. Now, is that an excuse? Does it make it right? No, but I didn't have any other example. When you don't have someone to teach you, you go with what's in you, and let's face it, all of us have got some interesting stuff in us. Yes, that's a good thing; it helps to define where we really are. But when the vows you promised get tested, now we find out who we really are.

"OMG"
The Vows Get Tested

One thing that I have learned is that when people talk about for better or for worse, we tend to think to the left. The truth is that the events of our past don't always lean in the direction of worse. We all have some type of past. Yes, I agree, the feelings of pain last longer than euphoria, but when the pain stops, the memory of that euphoria is still incredible.

I had a past that was incredibly complex, and sometimes we come into a new relationship with feelings of euphoria masking the failures of that past. We bring the thoughts of all of the good things that we can now accomplish, and we come with false expectations that have carried over into this relationship. Or we come expecting this relationship to make our dreams come true. Good experiences help us grow; they help develop us and they give us a sense of success. They give us a sense of victory in our lives.

When you've ridden in a Bentley, it's very difficult to now ride the bus. When you've worn Cole Haan shoes, Payless just doesn't feel good. I personally have had the opportunity to minister with people all over the world. I've sung with such notables as Aretha Franklin, Ray Charles, and Tony

Bennett, and that's the short list. There were times when I had large amounts of money and was doing well and then there were times when I had nothing but the clothes on my back because of bad decisions. Sometimes we hope that we redeem what we lost in the past and we put that demand of assisting us to achieve that on the other person. We put that demand on our new precious spouses. We put that demand of recovery on people who had nothing to do with us losing it in the first place. We judge what they do and what they say and it's unfair and it's not godly, so we have to be careful when we talk about for better or for worse—we come with both. We come with the good. We come with the bad, we come with the indifferent, and yes, we come with the ugly.

I'm just like any other man. I hate failure, I hate not getting it right. When Adam lost in the Garden, the first thing he did was blame his wife. Not only did he blame her, he took a jab at God Himself! Adam's response to the inquiry of God was, "This woman, that YOU gave me, messed with that tree." In other words, it's her fault and it's your fault for making her in the first place! He didn't think about the consequences of his disobedience. The truth is that nobody gets it right all the time, but sometimes we come into a relationship expecting others to look at us in a right perspective all the time, even when the wrong speaks up, when the past shows our ugly side. That's when we go into that defensive mode or we switch on the denial mode—or we do both.

Either way, those things put strains on a relationship, but thank God for giving us a help-meet, who goes the Bible route, the God route, and commissions God's Spirit to fight for us.

A wife that is willing to fight for me. Yet, at the same time chooses not to get indifferent with me. One who says I'm going to get in here in the mud with you so we can get clean together. For me, I was finally able to stop the lies, stop the distrust, and stop the intimidation tactics I was using to take the attention off of my need to trust and my need to admit that I needed help. Yes this is for better or worse at its core— at its best.

Even when it comes down to richer or for poorer, we have issues. We often come into a relationship with assets, money, and influence, and we sometimes have a tendency to lord that over our mate. Hey, we're trying to make an impression, and rightfully so. Hey, let's keep it 100 again, nothing looks better than a male peacock, with a full-color spread and a strut to match! You know, the lion with that dark full mane and that "don't mess with me" gait. Tony Powell, 6'2", Bertini two-piece, Brooks Bro. Cashmere mock neck, Mezlan baby Crocodiles, Rolex two-tone Submariner, platinum box-link bracelet, Lincoln Town Car.

My momma told me as a young man, she said, "Boy! You are big and you are going to draw attention to yourself, if they're gonna look, let them say, 'My God, he sure is big, but he's sharp, isn't he!'" Having money and things are good, the Bible actually says that money answers all things: Ecclesiastes 10:19. People say money can't buy you happiness, true, but it can make you HAPPY!

Oh come on now, tell the truth; have you ever had a pocket full of money and been with people you really enjoy and not been happy? Of course not! Besides, the truth of the matter

is, whatever you have, according to the Word of God, after those vows, now belongs to them, and whatever they have now belongs to you. For many relationships, this is a battleground that is the second-largest destroyer of marriages, period. And in a number of cases, when it comes to money, it becomes a competitive event instead of a team event.

I told you my situation was complex. One instance was that my wife made more money than I did—not a little bit more, but a whole lot more—maybe $80,000 a year more. Well, that doesn't necessarily make a man feel real good, does it? Mr. "Big-Baller" was rolling marbles in comparison to my wife. I'm supposed to be the head of the house, you know: the number one "supply-guy." Head means serving, head means I'm the supporter, not just the provider, and God tells us in his Word that when you think you're the one providing, it's actually Him. God said, "I will supply. I will provide all of your needs according to my riches and glory by Christ Jesus."

When I came into my relationship with my wife, I did not have anything. I was actually surprised she even considered talking to me after she found out just how broke I was, and I thanked God I had an anointing, because I didn't have anything else. I will say that I was quite intriguing, quite the communicator, very intellectual, and yes, large, but cute (stop hatin'). Aside from this, the truth of the matter is that this woman took a huge risk because no woman looks at a man that doesn't have anything tangible to bring to the table. In retrospect, I have to believe that at some point she wondered if she was crazy. I never asked, but in my mind, I know it's true.

Entering into a relationship with monetary insecurity issues puts you on the defensive as a man right off the bat, and that's where I was. I didn't want to discuss money. I didn't want to give up any money, I wouldn't receive money, and half of the time; I didn't have any money to give up. And so there I was, literally having to learn humility, battling my pride, having to learn how to let my guard down. You see, most of my life I have worked either in the music industry or in the ministry industry. Both industries were on fire in the eighties and nineties. I did a lot of work in the jingle business, and I made some good money, but I did not manage it well and so easy come…well, you know the rest.

I also worked in ministry, which means you really got paid based on how people's mindsets were about what God was doing and blessing them or how much money they had. You were expected to just say, "Well, praise the Lord, whatever you have." That's what I'll accept. It was the "Church Work Hustle." That mindset did not help when it came down to paying bills, being a provider, and eventually because ministry business is often like the sales business. It is not always the most solid business to be in; I often ended up out of one job and then to another very quickly. In my case, trying to follow God ended up almost breaking me. I don't blame that on God at all.

Another problem was that I was a part-time tither. That's right, I believed in tithing, when it was convenient. I believed in tithing when I had a little bit more than I wanted to have so that it didn't hurt so bad, but when those times came for the tithe, I went to the escape saying "the Lord loves a cheerful giver, and I wasn't happy, so don't give!"

But thank God I had a wonderful wife who was willing to actually help love the "hell" out of me, literally. Now it was never violent or hostile, but God, I'm a man with a strong will—no, I mean REALLY strong. I'm telling you, Dr. Ruby E. Powell has an "S" under her blouse on her chest and this woman could not break this will of mine. She could not crack it, nor could she bend it. You see, a man's will is directly connected to his strength. A man's strength is his badge of honor; to me the words weak and man are like oil and water; they just don't mix. But she found a way to love through it, and that same love broke it—no, it destroyed it.

When the Word of God tells you that love conquers everything, it really does, and eventually you get to a place where you find out a little something that I will talk about later in this book. Love, real love becomes a who in your life and not a just a what.

You've heard many times that love is an action word—that it's a verb. Well, guess what? Love is one of those words that has two literary definitions. It's not just a verb, but it is a noun, and a proper noun at that. Yes, God said He is Love and that He was the example of it. Not that He was the picture of it, not that He was the prototype of it, but that He was the origin of every atribute we know and acknowledge as love. Eventually, in your relationship, you get to the place where love is no longer just what you do or what you say, or what you have, or even what you believe, but you eventually get to the place where you will see and experience God Himself through your spouse. You find out that no person could love us through all of the craziness that we do, except God did it through the them.

5

It Comes Down
To Choices

Our past shows us ourselves. We see characteristics and traits that we had as children, as youth, and as young adults. There is denial, hurt, and deceit, and those habits and those bad ways ease their way out in our relationships. Not only that, but we find a way to validate it. We find a way to dismiss the fact that things are not right and get okay with it. We get complacent about addressing it, and before you know it, when you get into a relationship and the blissful part of those vows that say to have and to hold started to come down to the next line. For better or for worse, that's when you get to see all the colors of your personal rainbow come out—and they are not all so bright.

As a young man, my reality was family discord and the pain of being rejected by my father. Here at this junction of pain is where I learned that it was easier to believe lies instead of truth. So guess what, I became quite a little white liar. Well, not actually white, and the lies were really quite big. Nevertheless, I convinced myself that they weren't really large; they were just adjustments to the truth.

When you're in relationship and you come out of that blissful

time of "to have and to hold" and you hit the doors of "for better or for worse," when the worst comes up, you'll be surprised how much you will reach back into the bag of the past and pull out some of those old habits. You don't intend to, but like I said, if you don't speak of your past, your past will speak of you.

Our marriage began to hit the doorway of difficult times financially. I was not a good disciplinarian, and when it came to money, I would simply deceive myself. I would pretend bills didn't exist, and I didn't want to talk about the fact that I didn't handle money well. Because of those bad habits, those lies about money, and the inability to pay bills on time, it created difficulty and problems for my marriage.

This wonderful wife of mine, in her hurt and disappointment, decided that rather than discard me, like I'd already done a couple of times before, she was going to live out our vows. Not just because she said them to me, but because she made those vows to God. Was it easy? Of course not, this woman got upset with me and did not have a problem letting me know that, but rather than discard me or throw me away, rather than enroll me in the "NN program" (the NN stands for "No Nookie"), she decided she would pray and seek the counsel of her God as well as her pastor, Momma Jo Ann Long to help her focus the energy on not retaliating but restoring, helping me get back to being the man of God that I was supposed to be.

She did not shut down on me or give up on me, but instead she prayed for me. She talked to me, she supported me in my efforts to change bad habits into good ones, to change

an ugly past into a brighter future. Why? Because if she could get her man to lead in an earnest and honest and a righteous way, it was going to produce for her and our entire household, and she knew that her prayers and her effort helped me to get over that hurdle, where I was always ashamed of my financial abilities. You see, there was a time when I had lots of money, but I didn't manage it well, and when you don't manage what you have well, you don't get much more. Just ask the three talent recipients.

But I blame her for this more than anything. She helped me to know that integrity was more important than stuff. You see, I finally got it. When God created woman in the garden for man, he did not call her his bed toy. He did not call her his sidekick, and he definitely did not call her his slave. He called her a help-meet, a helper, someone to help him. Why? He knew man was going to need some help. I had to realize—and God helped me to do it—that I was not sleeping with the enemy, but the enemy was already very resident in my past. He was resident in my prior behavior, and because I covered him up and stuck him in a bag and pretended like it was just some old luggage, he forced his way out to try to destroy my third marriage. But it didn't work because I have a wife who was determined we were going to live these values out together and I was going to do my job. And if I did my job, God promised that he would do His job in me. And He did just that.

You see, it's pretty common knowledge that the first five years of marriage are the years of both bliss and of learning and discovery. I'd already been married twice, so the bliss thing was good, but it wasn't something that I hadn't been acquainted

with. Yes, it was different and it was awesome, but I had been there before. Not only is it a time of bliss, but it's a time of learning and discovery as well, and in my case, my discovery was one that challenged me a great deal. I have had some good jobs, made some good money, owned property, and had a lot of positive things happen. This was not one of those times. I had just come out of divorce number two, and I had come out literally with nothing more than my life and what few things I walked away with because it was a hostile situation. Yes hostile, violent—I mean, this wife thought her uncle was Mike Tyson, for real.

Now my parents were old school and taught me that a real man never puts his hands on a woman. Well, on a Sunday morning, after some very heated verbal and, yes, physical exchanges, "Mike-etta" decided to throw a couple of butcher knives in my direction for me to examine! When I came to myself, I was having a conversation with her knees, with my hand around her neck, three feet up against a wall! I knew at that moment that I could never see this woman again and that the marriage was history.

So now I come to this marriage with nothing more than desire, God in my heart, a few possessions, and that's it. To be honest, Ruby really didn't even need a husband. I'm telling you, this woman had it all together. She had a fantastic job, making more money by virtue of contracted salary than I ever made working on any one job. She had not one, but two degrees, working with Chicago State University on contract under her own conditions and on her own terms. She was also an executive supervisor for DCFS, with a staff of over 70 people. She already owned her own house. She

already owned her own car. She had a daughter in private school and ballet school, at the same time! The woman was on the board of directors of everybody's stuff except for Johnson and Johnson. She did not need a husband, or at least this was how I saw it. She came to the table with everything; I came to the table with what seemed to me to be nothing.

This, my friend, was a real battleground in the mind of this man. If you be honest, it would be in yours as a man too, but the fact still remains. This was still the best marriage of my life. This was the will of God for my life. So although in the natural I had to fight the issues, primarily pride and the lack of things I did not have, guess what? I had a wife who knew that when she came to the table and again was convinced she was anointed to be my wife, it was her fault that I took on the mindset that I could do better and be better. She never lorded it over me that she made more money than I did, that she had a house and I didn't, that she had a car and I didn't, that she had bank accounts with actual money in them and I didn't, or even that she had several degrees and I didn't. She never made me feel bad about any of those things. I did a good enough job of feeling sorry for myself on my own. Trust me, I beat up on myself like I'd stolen something from myself, but this was still the best time of my life. In every deficiency, God sees efficiency.

She did outclass me, but she did not outrank me, and she would be the first one to remind me of that. I was her king and her head. She knew that if she built in this man of God, if she could help me see who God had made me to be, that I would find it and I would make it there.

That's something I can blame on her. I point the finger at her because eventually I got through my pride issues and found out what God needed me to do for my rank sake, not my class sake. Let's make sure we learn this fellas: We Are not in this thing for just ranking class. God sets the rank. You determine the class based on how you perform through your rank, and rank is there based on what God says, to let the greatest view be the servant. I had to learn how to serve this woman that I love—not just tell her what to do, but also do it so she could see. I'm willing to show you what to do. It's a different world out here. When you put blame aside and start looking internally at yourself to see what it is you need to produce—what this marriage needs to not just work, but to grow in God.

So now let's look at where we are in the vows. We have already experienced, "to have and to hold" and we've enjoyed that. We have also explored "For better or for worse," as well as looking at the real perspective of "for richer, for poorer." But now we get to "in sickness and in health."

One thing is for certain: as we prepare to get married and enter into a life of love, bliss and family, the one thing that you don't spend a whole lot of time thinking about is being sick. Let's face it; if we've got a reasonable amount of functional health, sickness is not something we entertain in thought. We know we stay active, we stay busy, we try to stay healthy, we try to eat well, and even when we don't do all of those things, most of the time our level of sick is pretty much encompassed by a migraine headache, maybe a bad case of upset stomach and diarrhea. Maybe even the flu or something like that. But the truth of the matter is that one out of every

12 people gets hit with some type of a serious illness, sometimes even something that's life-threatening. Whether it's high blood pressure, diabetes, cancer, Parkinson's, or dementia, it can leave the person impaired physically for life.

It happens to family members, it happens to mothers and fathers, and yes, it happens to husbands and wives. When I got married, the only sickness or health issue I had was that I was as big as a building. I weighed in excess of 500 pounds, but I got around pretty well. Hey, not only that; but my wife loved musicians and big men. Hot Dang! Keno! Yahtzee!! I had both of those down. My doctor used to say, "Powell, outside of being as big as a house, you're as healthy as a horse." It is a fact that even concrete wears out after enough abuse and use.

After approximately 10 years of marriage, I started to experience deterioration in my joints and my spine. The weight had virtually destroyed the marrow in the bone and caused three discs in my spine to degenerate on one side. Before long I was not able to walk and to get around like I used too. Within two years I couldn't walk at all without a cane or rollator. I became immobile, and the weight situation along with the immobility created real problems. I became unable to work or even get around. I couldn't do any job that required me to stand longer than 15 minutes.

Now my physical ability was limited, and my income-making ability was limited as well. My ministry ability had limitations, and this affected my household in more ways than I could've imagined. With poor and limited mobility and now marginal health, my wife got an unwanted promotion from the primary

breadwinner to the only breadwinner. I had children who were young at that time, around 4, 6, and 8 years of age. I was supposed to look after and take care of them, but instead, they had to look after me. They had to help me to get things or pick things up or to put socks on. It was a total turn around, and that was a real challenge.

Let me be honest, it wasn't a challenge, it pissed me off and here's why. Imagine a wife who's working a full-time job for the state, supervising in excess of 95 staff. After leaving them, she had to come home to three young children who she had to nurture and educate, not neglecting quality time. She also had an NFP organization in its embryotic stages and was in the final year of a doctoral program via an online university. This "Superwoman" now had a husband that could hardly reach his shoes to put them on or get into a full set of clothing without help. Our vows were not only being tested—they were being tested to the max.

She never once complained. She never once showed anger or resentment to me. But I know how hard this had to be on her, and I was busy trying to figure out anything I could do to help her and not hurt her. When you're in those situations, you better thank God for a spouse who has determined that love is going to be about "who" and not just "what." My wife loves me, and I have no doubt about it. I don't even know if I could measure her love for me, but she loves God more than she loves me, and her efforts to please her God may have been the only thing to save not only my life, but our marriage as well.

We never reached a point of separation or even discussing divorce because the "D" word was not allowed in our house, nor in our conversation, but we had times that were extremely strenuous: relation-wise, emotion-wise, attitude-wise. There were times when we went through a number of days and we didn't say anything that was not totally necessary to be said. We never denied each other our rightful sexual needs, but the desire was diluted because of the challenges we both were living through. Yet, we never stopped praying, and we never stopped paying attention to God, even when we didn't want to look at each other. We had to love God fully, so that he could help us love each other, unconditionally.

Have you ever heard the saying, "It's gonna get worse before it gets better?" Well, needless to say; things got worse, and some very serious decisions had to be made. You see, they couldn't repair my knees without replacing my hips too. They couldn't replace my hips because I was too overweight for surgery compliance. I couldn't lose the weight because of limited mobility due to bad knees and hips, and in case you haven't noticed, I'm now in what is called, a vicious cycle! The decision was made that I would have surgeries not only for joint replacement, but also in weight reduction.

And so in 2012, I embarked upon not one, not two, not three, not four, but five major surgeries within the course of two and a half years. These were not easy or simple surgeries by any stretch of the imagination. The first one was Bypass Surgery so that I could break this vicious cycle. I had weight-loss surgery, which helped me to reduce enough to deal with the joints. That was difficult in itself and required a very

concise recovery regimen. After the surgery, I had to deal with eating correctly, mobility issues, weakness, nausea, and adjusting to new ways of eating. This created challenges for my wife. Why? Because I had to eat only certain foods. Well, I had a wife who worked, took care of the kids, and now had to fix a specific menu for me to eat so that this could be successful. Fortunately, I have an older daughter.

My daughter Adya helped so much, and I think without even knowing it, she helped to keep my wife from losing her mind at times. Never was there an issue about her love because it stayed focused in the direction that it had throughout this time. She loved God more than she even loved me, praise God! After healing thoroughly from the surgery and losing weight—145 pounds to be exact—the doctors were now ready to begin the process of joint replacement.

I currently have a plaque on the wall of the St. James Hospital, that says I am the first male joint replacement recipient to endure not one, not two, not three, but all four of my primary joints replaced within a two and a half year period. Now you may not think that's a big deal, but I promise you, taking an entire knee out, putting a new one in, one that is made of titanium alloy and polymer, and then sewing it up and getting that person into therapy to make that joint work is a whole lot of challenge.

It didn't just happen once. It had to happen four times. Yes, I have had both hips and both knees replaced. My wife had to endure a staph infection, next-day therapy, my screeching in pain, "fetch this," "get that," "help me here," "wash me there," "pick this up"—oh my God! She did this for two and

a half years while maintaining a full-time job, raising three young children all under the age of 12, looking after our home, and maintaining ministry while pursuing a doctorate degree. Who does that? My wife does, and not only did she do it, she did it well. Now you want to talk about somebody who took their vows seriously. That woman who I blame for my well-being, for my change in attitude, for my integrity, for the increase in my physical wellbeing—I blame her because somehow she found a way to love God enough so that when everything challenged these vows, she maintained and stayed in the battle.

Now I'm bragging a lot about my queen, but I'm going to pat myself on the back a little bit too. It was not an easy task, enduring five surgeries and four sets of therapy to better myself, but I've valued my queen so much that I knew if I could just get healthy, if I could just redeem the time, if the power of prayer is never to be underestimated. Not only the power of prayer, but the power of listening to wisdom and counsel.

6

Our Criteria Became The Word of God

You already know I had an incredible spiritual mother in Dr. Jo Ann Long. But what you didn't know until now is that my natural birth mother was pretty incredible herself. Her name was Elouise Powell, and she was the best mother in the world to me. Momma was one of those women who was well trained as a child. She was an incredible cook, kept an immaculate house, washed, line-dried, ironed, folded and or hung up clothing for a husband and three kids, and yes took us to church every Sunday. Both of these incredible women experienced heart-crushing challenges in their marriages and yet serviced, honored, and loved their husbands until the end, which for one was divorce and for the other terminal illness.

These two mothers, even through pain and eventually death, one natural the other emotional, were both able to help me to understand that not only should I, but that I really could love my wife, like Jesus loved His Church. Now, in my season of medical and physical deficiency, I can see what I have, maybe for the first time ever. Love has become a "who" and not just a "what"! The Bible is clear: God is Love—not God produces love, or God exemplifies Love, but God, He is Love.

When you've been through hell and you've got the scars to show for it, and the Love, that is God, brings you out, you have a new and different appreciation for the vessel that He uses to show Himself. I saw the Love that is God in my wife, and I cried—no, I wept. Why weep you say? When all your masculinity means absolutely nothing without the help, the care, the love, the dedication, the resolve . . . do I really need to go on! If I could just get my mobility back, I knew I could do everything I needed to help take care of her, by "vowing up," and yes, that opportunity did come.

Now, was this time easy? Of course not. Trust me, as I stated earlier, whatever's in you is going to come out, and a lot of things that were deeply embedded in me had to come out my insecurities, my shortcomings, my lethargy, and my self-denial. I had to face all of this, and I had to try to make amends for it the best way I could by asking God to forgive me, ask my wife to forgive me, and then change my behavior.

Our vows were severely tested, but guess what, we weren't the first and we wouldn't be the last. Everybody's vows get tested in some way or other. The levels of testing are different, and the circumstances are different, but the outcome is usually the same, a grade is issued. We either pass or fail the test. You see, we didn't make our vows just to each other, but when we said "for better, for worse, for richer, for poorer, in sickness and in health, til' death do us part," we were also promising God we would do these things: until we are no longer alive to fight this battle together, until we are no longer breathing to believe God. That He would fix whatever's broken, to repair whatever was not functioning properly, to replace whatever was not there anymore; to restore whatever

had been lost. You see, that's what marriage is really about.

It's the story of God's love and restoration played out in the lives of two people. Two people who love each other. You see, John 3:16 is not just a poetic quotation, nor is it just to sound eloquent. It means what it says. For God so loved the world that he gave the best and most precious thing he had, JESUS, who was Love in human form. That whoever believed in this Love would not ever perish but have life forever. This thing applies to relationships. It applies to the covenant of marriage.

For Tony Powell so loved God and Ruby that he gave the best qualities of his life. He gave his service. He gave his soul. He gave his yearning. He gave his protection, he gave his life to the best of his ability so that she could have eternal life, a life of prosperity, a life of wholeness, a life of richness, a life of fullness, a life of joy in this earthly realm, and will never perish but have life that way and better, even after this life.

That's what the blame game is all about. Where would I be without the wonderful wife that I blame for my good qualities? This woman that I blame for my well-being? This wife that has helped make me better than I was when I met her? The person that I blame for helping me increase in ways that I would have never been able to do on my own. The queen of my life that helped me to learn that I'm better than I thought I was, that I'm not as bad as I insisted I was. Ruby helped me to see that I could do more than I thought I could do— that I could achieve the dreams that I had. The ones that I was convinced were just fairy tales and not real. Ruby believed that what the other relationships, my previous marriages,

produced that was negative and destructive had nothing to do with what God said concerning us now! Did that take some blood, sweat and tears? You better know it! But she asked God to help her see me as dirt! I hear you laughing again—yes, dirt! But when someone else treats us like dirt, all they get is dirty themselves. But God, and yes my Ruby, saw more than dirt—they saw soil! What's the difference? I'm glad you asked. You see, dirt is usually filled with debris and byproducts that prohibit anything ever to live in that soil except weeds.

On the other hand, soil is full of nutrients, potassium, niacin, and iron, and if you're smart enough to plant some seeds in it, dare to shine a little sunshine on it, and water it, guess what, it's going to produce something good. It may produce some flowers, something that is beautiful and fragrant, bring pleasure and enjoyment to others, or perhaps it will produce some type of fruit: something that nourishes, flavors, and provides pleasure to others. Not to mentions both flowers and fruit produce seeds, to reproduce themselves.

Wow! In every area of relationship and marriage that I failed not once, but twice before, I know I had victory and incredible success. You see, that's the blame game—the right way. Not because she did something to hurt me, but she did something that helped me. Not because she did something to knock me down but because she did everything to lift me up. And guess what happened? I was now driven to do the same thing for her. You see, there are only two things that predominantly helped us to produce the type of marriage that makes people ask us, "What are you guys doing? What is your secret?" Here is what our secret is. There are two things.

Number one, we made the criteria of our marriage the Word of God. We set our baseline around what God's Word says, first about us as individuals and secondly about what God says about us as a couple. My opinion is just like your opinion; we all have one. But our opinions are based on our past, our history, our knowledge, our experiences, and we've seen previously in this book where all of those things come from.

They come from places we didn't want to acknowledge were there. They come from baggage that we had no desire to bring with us, or in some cases didn't even know we had. Nevertheless, this is what we based our previous criteria on: things we've experienced in our past, and that's never good. All those things are based on areas of mistake, areas of misinformation, areas of failure, areas of frustration.

You don't want to build anything on a foundation of the things that went wrong. You have to build your foundation blocks on something that will not shake, that will not give way, and the only thing that we know of that is unshakable and unmovable is God's Word. He said Heaven and Earth would pass away before even a word that he's said fails. He said "I, God; watch over my Word, I personally make sure that everything there comes to pass."

Your parents do the best job they can, but they're human just like you and they made mistakes just like you did. You don't want to build anything of value on a foundation of mistakes, so He must be your criteria, the Solid Rock, the Word of God. Everything that we need is found in God's Word. I don't mean sitting around waiting for some deep, reverberating voice to speak to you in the middle of the night. I'm not

talking about running to everybody's prophetic line to get some kind of fortune-like word. I'm sorry, the Bible still works just fine on its own, and in there you will find answers to every issue of life, but you don't want to wait till the issues start to use the criteria; you want to use the criteria before the issue starts. It's called preventive preparation. Getting the answers before you even need them. How do you do that? The Word of God says, "If you spend time seeking me in my word, I will be found. Now something incredible is about to happen, Love becomes a "Who" and not just a "what."

All of the answers as to how to get marital problems fixed were found in God's Word, and so are yours. "But we had communication issues." We found solace in the Word of God: "Come let us reason together." Let's talk it out together. "Don't let the sun go down on your wrath." I'm paraphrasing, but all of these things can be found in the Bible. The more you let the Word of God become your criteria, the more you learn. Emotional issues no longer weaken the building blocks of your marriage. They are no longer weakened by shortcomings or opinions. They are strengthened by the mortar of the Spirit of God and because you are building together based on promises that you made both to each other and to God.

Now guess what you've done. You've now brought God into the picture to have to see to it that things work because you have kept him tightly in the mix of your house. He promises that you are not just valuable to each other, but you're valuable to me. So now, I vow to you; that if you follow my Word, that if you obey my Word, you will see the good fruit and the fruit of the land will be yours. And so first we made the criteria of our marriage, of our raising our children, of how

we handle our money, of our relationship intimately and sexually—even every aspect of our relationship. We found our blueprint for the way. It's not always the best way, but we start with better and work our way to best. We could find a better way to do things, and those things had to work because if they didn't, the failure factor wasn't on us, it would be your God.

So now we can't point fingers at each other and blame and we can't point fingers at each other and take the credit. We have to point fingers at God and his Word.

It makes God happy, and the union that He sees in us brings him joy because if we're doing what we're designed to do, it's going to spill out on people like you via this book, and on people we're around and share with via our faith and our love for each other. The second way that we managed to see to it that this thing works is that we have what we call our 4-B Principle.

Our 4-B Principle
For Marriage & For Life

We have a system that we call the 4-B Principle for our marriage and our life. It is what some would call an oxymoron in that it is both "Spiritual and yet practical." We have committed to putting this system into practice every single day, and I'm telling you the truth, since its inception, I can count on one hand the times we've ever had anything more than an "energetic vocal disagreement." Let's take a look.

Number 1: Be prayerful.

We have found that we can get so much more done when we take the time to pray together. Not just praying for each other, not just praying about each other, but praying together. We set time. We try to every day. I won't lie, sometimes we don't make it every day, but whenever we think about it and we're together, whether it is in bed, or in the car or in the grocery store parking lot, we stop, take a moment and talk to God, together. Once we started dedicating time to pray together as a couple, we did not start with elegant conversation. In fact, we started with some basic "Hello God," "How you doin?" "Can you help us?" stuff. We prayed the very basics, but those prayers not only started to increase in us, but it

increased in others around us. You see, in the garden, it did not start with Adam and his woman together. It started with God and Adam together. It started with man and God and their relationship. They talked together every day in the cool of the evening. That was their prayer time. When the woman came in, they spent time talking to God. That was their prayer time.

That still exists to this day in our life. We saw more changes in our behavior, in our attitudes, in our relationship and our intimacy and our money matters and everything else. When we committed that we would pray for each other and not prey on each other—that we would not give Him, God a whole bunch of complaints about "she did this" or "he did that"—instead we'd go to God saying, Father, we both need you and we want You to love the "hell" out of us, and that's exactly what He's done.

Our marriage got so much better, in every area. Our communication got better, our finance management got better, care and character got better, our sex got better, our problem identification and resolution even got better. I know you're thinking "all this because of prayer?" No. All this because of praying together. Now, let's keep it 100, we had to be patient, because nothing of value happens overnight. Nothing. Patience is a requirement.

Number 2: Be Patient

Patience is something that is needed in every area of marriage. To see change it's needed. To produce fruit it's needed. To grow and develop it's needed. To be able to stay there and

fight it out. Patience is not something that God is going to just make happen. Patience is a work that you have to let happen thoroughly in your life. We had to learn that. I'm not going to be able to get over the little things that she does that drive me crazy overnight, and guess what, there are still some things she does that I don't think aren't ever gonna change. I have the patience to learn how to live with that and to put that in the column of little minor stuff that ain't such a big deal.

Number 3: Be pro-active.

We can't be reactionary. Being reactionary is not a good thing because anything that reacts usually has volatile results. Something is going to blow up when there's an action, if there's some type of a chain reaction or reaction it is usually explosive. You don't want to just be apathetic, but you want to be pro-active. You want to move forward on a thing and not wait till it blows up—till you get to the point where you don't wait for your wife to say, "Well, what's wrong with you?" Just put it out there. I don't wait for my wife to ask, "What happened to the money?" I speak up and say what happened to the money. I don't wait for my wife to say, "Did you intend on cleaning this mess up?" I just start cleaning.

You have to be pro-active because there is no problem, there is no difficulty, there is no challenge that we can't together overcome and we can together find the answer to. What if we sit back waiting on the other person to fix it, to change it, to do something about it, to say something about it, to pay for it, to ignore it, to build it? If we wait for that, guess what ended up in pro about that at all. Now you're going

from pro to post accurate and that's gonna be real volatile because all of that is full of explosive element. Something's gonna blow up and that is never good and lastly, be permanent. That's right.

Number 4: Be permanent.

The last part of those vows says until death do us part. Folks, divorce is not an option. It is not a conversation or word that's even permitted in my house.

I vowed to stick with this woman through everything, and she vowed to stick with me. I promised that to her, but I also promised to God. This is a permanent matter. I'm not going out of this. I'm not running from this. I'm not trying to escape this. I didn't marry the wrong person. I got the right one because I vowed to have the right one, and if it wasn't right when I did it, God has the power to make it right because I've committed to staying in this thing permanently. There is no aspect of it not being permanent.

This is for keeps. This is for life. This is forever, and if it's going to be forever, we might as well point the finger and say, "Hey, guess what? I'm staying with you. Whether you like it or not, it's your fault I'm here and I'm standing, but this fault is a good thing because it's your fault for loving me. Your fault for caring about me so much, for building me all the time for big encouragement, for loving God and seeking his word on how to be better yourself so that together we are more powerful than anything could imagine." Because if one can the set 1000 to flight, two can set 10,000. Look what we have the ability to do if we just believe.

The story closes,
but the journey continues

This book is the first published endeavor by me and my wife. It was done uniquely, in that outside of the chapter assignments, we did not collaborate in what we endeavored to share and, hopefully, give our insight on. If you haven't flipped this book over yet, you're in for a pleasant surprise. We have been programmed to find someone to blame, rather than to see the good in all things and give some credit where it is due. Life really does teach us that whatever we achieve or accomplish that is of any real value, somebody helped us.

In the case of my marriage and family, I blame my wife, Dr. Ruby E. Powell, the greatest thing to happen to me since salvation. It is my sincere prayer that something I've shared in this story of my life will give you both encouragement and hope for a wonderful marriage, whether it be from this day forward or perhaps in the future if you're not married yet. God created marriage, he blessed marriage, he loves marriage, and he keeps marriage, so long as you both shall live. I conclude with an actual letter of encouragement I wrote to my queen. With pen in hand and tears in my eyes, I shared this little thought with her, and now with you all.

A letter of encouragement for my queen.

The letter of encouragement that I wrote to my Queen . . .

My Dearest Queen,

It's difficult to write a letter of encouragement to someone who is has spent their life being a master encourager. For the 15 years that we've been married, I've watched you overcome incredible odds and yet always keep a positive and strong confession. You did all these things. Even in your times of exhaustion, you find a way to encourage me, your children and everyone else. Unimaginable. I've watched you live your vows to God and me with absolute heartfelt love and dedication. During this pivotal time of your personal journey towards destiny, I simply want to encourage you to know that your Lord and your God, who has given you direction and insight to bless thousands, is with you and has promised never to leave you, and I promise the same thing.

I blame you for every area of success I experience. I try to say something to build you and encourage you every day of my life because I know if I can keep you smiling and encouraged, my life will continue to be what it is right now: simply awesome. Continue to know and remember that he, God, who

has begun this incredible work in you, is going to see to it that the perfect completion and it will happen. I am, because of you. It's all your fault!

With gratitude and enormous love,

Your priceless

Anthony Powell

Mr. Tony Powell is known as a Master Music Instructor, a Chicago grown product with over 35 years of musical history under his belt. He has taught music on three different levels to include master vocal instruction at two professional music institutions.

Tony started singing at the age of 11 and has sung professionally for over 25 years. Working in both the jingle and movie industry, Tony has extensive ministry experience as well. Tony has sung in ministry for such notables as Oral Roberts, R.W. Schaumbach, John O'Steen, Benny Hinn and many others. He has been Associate Pastor at three ministries. He has sang in 47 cities and 9 nations of the world.

Tony and Ruby are the parents of four dynamic children: Adya Monique, Kasiya Janae, Nathan Joseph Anthony, & Jonathan Christian. They along with their children have served in ministry for many years. They have all been bitten by the missions bug and look with anticipation to taking the gospel to every continent in the world!

FLIP THE SCRIPT
TO SEE WHY . . .

It's All
HER
Fault